M000013241

America

One Step at a Time

America

One Step at a Time

A 3,400 Mile Walk
in Search of America

by

Daniel Rogers

Thirsty Turtle Press
Bloomingdale, Ohio

All rights reserved. No part of this book may be reproduced or transmitted in any form or by any means, electronic or mechanical, including photocopying, recording or by any information storage and retrieval system, without written permission from the author, except for the inclusion of brief quotations in a review, which may be used with proper citation.

Second Printing 2015
Copyright ©2003 Daniel Lee Rogers

Thirsty Turtle Press

Email: Sheltowee99@gmail.com
www.sheltoweehikes.com

Edited by Dawn Marie Stringer and Nina Baxley Rogers
Maps by John Muse

ISBN 0-9729038-0-1
Library of Congress Control Number 2003091467

To the memory of my parents

Frank G. Rogers
Elaine A. Rogers

Acknowledgements

To chase a dream of this magnitude is not possible without the love and support of so many. I am humbled at the friendship I have received from so many, and grateful to those who have helped me to put this book into its finished form.

Thanks to my wife Nina Baxley Rogers, without her love and support, I would never have seen the Pacific Ocean. Thanks also to Anne Rogers, my wonderful daughter who brings me so much joy.

Thanks to Dodger and Nimblewill Nomad, who hiked with me so many miles. It was a joy, my friends.

Thanks to Kurt Russell and Wanderlust Gear for sponsoring me and providing me with world-class tents.

Thanks to my mom, Elaine Rogers, and to my brothers Frank, John, and Carl for their support and love.

Thanks to the Colgate Palmolive Corporation for fourteen wonderful years and for understanding me.

Thanks to Dawn Stringer for editing the manuscript, as well as for developing and maintaining my website.

Thanks to John Muse for his creation of maps in the book.

Thanks to Jaime Hilliard for the design of the Thirsty Turtle logo.

Thanks to George and Michelle Zavatsky and Ed Speer for their advice on publishing and their friendship.

Thanks to Honey and Bear at The Cabin in Maine for a great place to sit and relax and begin writing.

Thanks to Mrs. Gwen Baxley, Mr. Hugh Baxley and Megan and Stephen Monk for all their support.

Thanks to Gary Rosenlieb for all his technical support.

Thanks to John Young, Bob Moore, and Pat Duggan for their eternal friendship.

Thanks also to all the Scouts and fine folks at Boy Scout Troop 192, Don DuRussel, Karen Sousa, Earl Needham, Allan Stibora, Howard Jones, Mike Smith, Jeff Smith, Mary and Leon Ham, Brooks Kelly, and the scores of people I met along the way.

Foreword

Though our ranks are few, there certainly does exist (as Service so eloquently observed long ago), "...a race of men that don't fit in, a race that can't stand still..." We're a restless bunch, for sure, possessed by a strange yet mysteriously instinctive drive known simply as "wanderlust."

And so, inevitably, and as our wanderlust-driven lives go, on a warm August morn in 2001, my dear friend of like kinship, Dan "Sheltowee" Rogers—being the helpless victim that he was, so consumed by that smoldering fire burning ever-constant and deep within (and being of a seasoned nature, a backpacker)—stepped from his front porch in Ohio and walked across America!

Let me alert you right here, dear reader, for it is fact (as the old Nomad has alluded), "There is no land discovered that can't be found anew, so journey on intrepid, into the hazy blue..." Be warned! If you are one so driven—driven to escape the shackles of daily, mundane existence, if you are one endlessly tormented from within—tormented to the extent of abandoning all the senseless, dead-end, boring routines, routines imprisoning you to the very depth of your being, and if (as Thoreau has stated), "if you are ready to leave father and mother and brother and sister, and wife and child and friend, and never see them again...then you are ready for a walk." Ah yes, be warned, for as you depart on this spiritually life-changing odyssey with Sheltowee, you too will be driven to rise up and go.

And so, as you armchair-trek this exciting, heartwarming story about the people and places of this, our grand homeland, America, keep your soiled old pack and nubbed-off hiking sticks next your chair, so to grab them when the wanderlust swirls and erupts, striking from the depths of your restless soul to lift you; and as your shadow clears the door and you disappear down that adventuresome road, thence to fade, becoming "lost to the dust outward blown" take just a moment to mark your place and take this remarkably compelling, life-changing book along. For (as in the spirit of Tolkein), you will be gone for awhile. You see, "...The road goes ever on and on, down from the door where it began. Now far ahead the road has gone, and I must follow it if I can"

Ah yes, here's to the wanderlust in us all—and here's to you, Sheltowee, dear friend; keep chasing your dreams!

M. J. Eberhart
Author of Ten Million Steps
www.nimblewillnomad.com

Table of Contents

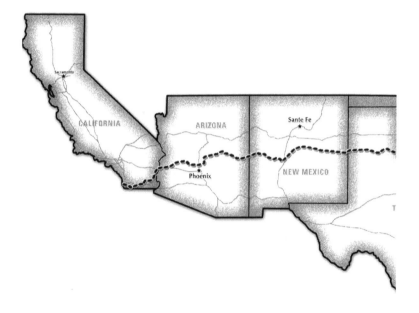

Dreaming

I stood in the brisk wind atop Mount Katahdin, tears welling up in my eyes, surrounded by friends, each of us overwhelmed with emotion as the champagne bottle passed from hand to hand. I looked in awe at the beauty of the Maine wilderness, which lay some 4,000 feet below me. On top, here in the alpine zone, there were no trees and the weather was harsh, even on a good day.

For five and a half months I had been known as "Sheltowee". I had lived life freely, roaming through the eastern forests, slowly making my way through each of the fourteen states that comprise the most famous trail in the world. At times I had to walk a mile out of my way just to get water, having given up the luxuries that go with "civilized" life. I had endured many hardships, including walking miles in the rain and snow, and dealing with the oppressive summer heat. That summer along the Appalachian Trail, however, had been the most rewarding summer of my life.

The hike was not easy, mentally or physically. I had lost nearly fifty pounds, as the mountains had worked my thirty-six-year-old body harder than it had even been worked before. But I had reached the end, the glorious summit of Mount Katahdin.

Two years later, I sat at the desk in my small factory office with the smell of deodorant brewing just outside my door. I was again thinking back, not only to Katahdin, but to nearly every day I had spent that summer, the internal struggle between high and low continuously raging in my mind, months after I had returned from the journey. I could not get it out of my system. I longed to go back, even though deep down I knew—you can't go back.

Colgate-Palmolive had been a great employer for fourteen years, and I had no complaints with my job. However, I longed for the freedom I had left behind on that mountain summit. I was weary of sitting in the busy New Jersey traffic, weary of sitting inside the factory day after day. I wanted, and more importantly, I needed adventure.

I began research, gathering maps of hiking trails all across the country, linking them together and creating a route. It was crazy talk; it made no sense to give up a secure job. It made no sense to give up the fourteen years in the company, to lose my retirement package and the financial security I enjoyed.

It made even less sense to me to live only for the purpose of going to work each day and return home to rest up for another day at the office. I debated the dilemma and decided that while the cost of chasing dreams was very high—the cost being failure, for we will never achieve all we set out to do—the reward was even greater. The reward was *life* as opposed to mere existence, and I was tired of merely existing. I wanted to <u>live</u> again.

I called several friends, and their support was incredible, letting me know that dreams are indeed made to chase, and if I could not get it out of my head, perhaps chasing that dream was just what I needed to be doing.

I called my friend Dodger and told him I was considering a great adventure, to walk across America, to leave the beaten path and go see the country, each state one by one. I figured it would take six years to cover over twenty thousand miles.

A few days later he called me back and asked if I would mind if he came along. I readily agreed and the decision to go was made.

The day I resigned from work was difficult. I had to hold back tears of emotion as I walked into my boss's office to drop a bomb on his otherwise routine day.

"Greg, I um—well, I need to give you my two weeks notice."

"What? You're kidding right? You're not quitting."

"Yes, Greg, I am really quitting, I ..."

"Who hired you? Why?"

"Nobody hired me; hell, if I wanted to work, I would stay here."

It was a shock to him, the company, and to me; I had actually quit my job.

Dodger traveled from his home in Oklahoma east to New Jersey to help me pack up my apartment. I had some old furniture that was not worth moving back to my hometown in Ohio. I planned to load it into my van, one piece at a time and take it to Goodwill. Dodger recommended just setting it out in the yard of the apartment complex; he was sure it would not last long. I was sure he was crazy but decided to give it a shot.

Early one Saturday morning we carried out the couch, then returned to the second-floor apartment to get a chair. Before we returned, a man was looking the couch over. He carried the stuff away as fast as we could bring it down.

He asked if I needed any newspaper for packing. I assured him I would not need any, that I was all set. About fifteen minutes later he returned, two boxes full of newspapers in his arms.

"Here, buddy. I know you're going to need these, so I brought them over anyhow. Thanks a bunch for the furniture."

He left and I sat in my empty apartment with Dodger and my friends Jeannie and Dawn, who had also come to help with the packing project. I laughed as I realized I had just traded all of my furniture to a stranger for a box of old newspapers. The four of us laughed heartily, rejoicing in the moment.

The next morning, Dodger and I headed for Ohio, with all that I still owned crammed into my Dodge Caravan. We would spend a few days visiting with my mom before starting our great adventure.

Ohio

After months of preparation, the time to walk out the door had finally arrived. I had prepared at length, studying maps and reading everything I could find about the many trails crossing America. Six years, forty-eight states, and twenty-four thousand miles lay ahead of me. America was waiting.

I had slept well and was refreshed and ready to go. Dodger and I, along with my brother, Carl, enjoyed my mom's breakfast of fried eggs and home fries, an old favorite. I didn't expect another home-cooked meal for some time, as I would literally be living on America's highways, back roads, and trails. With breakfast over, I hugged Carl and my mother Elaine good-bye, shouldered my pack, and took a last look at the small patch of land that my father had left me when he died. It was shortly after eight o'clock, and Dodger and I were on our way. We hiked off the porch and out of the valley in the late August morning heat, climbing the biggest hill we would see in several days.

After an hour of hiking, we were in the small, familiar town of Bloomingdale, Ohio. In many ways, this town is home to me; I attended grade school here, and I also served as the local Boy Scout leader for twelve years. On the west edge of town, I noticed the largest catalpa tree that I had ever seen. The heart-shaped leaves were at least as big as my hand, and the tree stood taller than the sizable farmhouse beside it. The trunk was bulky and would take three men to get their arms around it. It was covered with the long, cigar-shaped fruit that is its annual bounty. I had never noticed this tree before, even though I'd driven by it hundreds of times on my way to work, to scout meetings, and to the post office. In all those busy years, I'd never noticed it was a catalpa. The great thing about walking is that you get to see, feel, and experience the world around you. You don't get that so much on a bike, and you certainly don't get it in a car. In noticing this catalpa, I could tell that I was already seeing this town with different eyes—a wanderer's eyes—and not those of a man who had lived here practically all his life.

As a tourist on foot, I was visiting a part of Ohio that once thrived from the bustling coal and steel industries—the Steel Belt, now known as the Rust Belt. Bloomingdale is one of numerous small towns that have dwindled from prior prominence. It is now merely a suburb of the larger town of Steubenville, some fifteen miles to the east. A similar suburb is the village of Hopedale, which was the next stop on our hike across America. In Hopedale, we stopped at a local pub that I had frequented over the years. In this familiar setting, Dodger and I had a bite of lunch and a couple beers to celebrate our first day of hiking.

We marveled at the fact that we were already a curiosity, even though we'd barely hiked eight miles of the planned 24,000. Passing cars slowed down as people looked at us, and more than one pedestrian stopped to ask us where we were headed. Everyone we talked to seemed impressed, not just because we were hiking across the country, but because we had walked eight whole miles down Route 22! Dodger and I felt that we had earned little credibility yet, and that people should not be impressed with us … yet. Eight miles is not a great distance for a long-distance hiker, and the terrain was relatively easy. Plus, we were carrying particularly light packs, having worked diligently to reduce our pack weight for this journey. The average backpacker carries more than 40 pounds over more challenging terrain than Dodger and I would encounter on our first day. We each carried less than 20 pounds over the roads—an easy load, and an easy trail, for two seasoned hikers. Still, everyone else seemed amazed at the modern-day hoboes road-walking the gentle terrain of Ohio. When I saw these reactions, I realized something: not only was I seeing my hometown differently, but my old friends and neighbors were seeing *me* differently as well.

Around 3:00 that first day, we reached the Greenwood Cemetery and the gravesite of my father, Frank Rogers. Here, Dodger left me alone for a while so I could pay my respects. My father's passing away seven months before had been a major factor in my decision to attempt this hike. I remembered the summer evening in 1998 when I told my dad of my dream to thru-hike the Appalachian Trail.

"Are you going to quit your job?" he asked, concerned that this might be a foolish dream to chase.

"I don't know," I replied. "I hope not."

"For God's sake, Daniel," he said, clearly worried. "You can't quit your job."

As it turned out, I didn't have to quit my job. I was able to chase that dream and suffered no threat to my job security.

Then, on a cool Thanksgiving Day in 2000, I told him of my dream to hike across America and shared with him my meticulously developed plans.

"Are you sure you can afford this? You're sure the math is right?" he asked.

"I checked it three times, Dad."

"Then," he slowly replied, "I think you should chase your dream."

Six weeks later he was gone, the victim of a third and final heart attack. My father's death showed me that I am indeed mortal, and that I have only so much time to do the things in life I feel are important. My dear friend and fellow long-distance hiker, Eb "Nimblewill Nomad" Eberhart, has a saying that really hits home with me now: "When you're young, your 'one-of-these-days' list is pretty short, and you have all the time in the world. As you grow older, it seems your list gets longer and longer while your time grows shorter and shorter. Best start working on that list while you're young." I felt good, knowing that I was working on that list with my father's blessing. I knew that it was the right time for me to begin this hike.

Our first day ended in Cadiz, Ohio, another familiar town to me. We spent the night at the home of my friends, Scott and Donna Pendleton. I was happy to reach this first destination; the hot afternoon pavement had taken a toll on my soft feet, and I was ready for some rest.

I had grown up camping and hiking with Scott, and his home was a fitting place to spend my first night. His neighbor was having a pig roast, so we all walked down the street for dinner.

Early the next morning it was already warming up when we left Cadiz. I had underestimated the potential for foot problems when road-walking, and today looked to be another tough day of walking on hot pavement. I tried to focus less on my aching feet and more on today's goal: Fort Steuben Scout Camp near Deersville, Ohio, where we were to meet my old Boy Scout troop. The road led us through the reclaimed strip mine areas of Harrison County—the rusted ghosts of the Steel Belt. With the lack of scenery, it was difficult not to concentrate on my feet, which were swollen and blistered, slowing our pace considerably. After fourteen miles of painful walking, I was glad to see

Deersville. Here we found the Scouts, along with my twelve-year-old nephew, Frankie, ready to walk a bit of the journey with us. This reunion, along with a stop for homemade ice cream, gave my spirits a much-needed lift. The trail itself now changed from hot pavement to dirt road—much easier terrain for my weary feet. This was the Buckeye Trail. It led our little group directly to the Boy Scout camp property. These hills hold great meaning for me; it was here that I first set up a tent as an eleven-year-old Boy Scout. I spent many days and nights here as a youth, learning about nature and outdoor skills as I matured from an awkward Tenderfoot to a confident Eagle Scout.

The Scouts I hiked with also held great meaning for me. I had watched many of them transform from young Tenderfoots to the upper ranks of Scouting as well—following in my footsteps, much as they did now as we strolled down the dirt road that was the Buckeye Trail. I'd remained a registered member of the troop and had accompanied these boys on many outings in recent years. As a man who had long been a role model for the Boy Scouts in the area, I was proud that we were all together as I began chasing a new dream. I hoped that they would see my example and understand that being an individual and chasing dreams is okay, even if it means doing something out of the ordinary, like hiking across the country. I emphasized this during the afternoon Scout ceremony that was held.

When I awoke the next morning at the Scout camp, I knew I was in trouble. My body felt like it had been beaten, and it was a challenge just to stand on my tender, blistered feet. Most of my hiking in the past had been on trails, not roads, and pavement was much tougher on my feet than I had imagined. In addition, I hadn't hiked much in the preceding months. Dodger, having already completed a thousand miles that summer on the Appalachian Trail, had

no problems—his feet were rough and tough. Mine,
however, were soft and tender. I walked gingerly out of
camp to rejoin the Buckeye Trail, which would be our home
for most of the hike through Ohio. The 1,300–mile Buckeye
Trail encircles the entire state of Ohio and is marked by blue
blazes on trees, telephone poles, and other roadside objects
that can serve as markers.

The days through Ohio warmed up quickly, and the
late summer air was heavy with humidity. The countryside
was a mixture of hardwood forest, pastureland, and crop
fields. The rural roads led us past houses and farms, and
along the tall rows of corn and other crops. We walked
beneath the shade of the diverse population of hardwood
trees in the area. One of the houses we passed was home to a
friendly dog—so friendly, in fact, that it wanted to join us on
our hike across America! Up the lane it came, followed
shortly by a young girl, who obviously was chasing it.
Dodger and I helped her corral the dog, and she took it back
home. Sixty seconds later, the dog was back, its heart set on
at least taking a morning stroll with us. The girl again gave
chase. We laughed and chased—or played, from the dog's
point of view—until we caught him again. This bit of
excitement over, we bid the young girl a good day and
ambled on down the country road.

My feet grew tougher day by day and we soon found
ourselves in the small town of Old Washington, which was
one of the first areas of Ohio to be settled by westward-
bound pioneers. One route they followed was Zane's Trace.
Built in the 1790s, the footpath was rugged and not fit for
travel by wagons. It led west from Wheeling, in what was
then the state of Virginia, through present-day Zanesville,
Ohio, and south to Maysville, Kentucky, and eventually all
the way to Nashville, Tennessee. The Trace was used by
those returning on foot from New Orleans and Natchez after

floating their goods down the river to be sold at the ports along the Mississippi River. Settlers and missionaries also used this route in their efforts to bring salvation to the Indians of the Ohio frontier.

Old Washington is also remembered as the site of a skirmish between the Union army and General John Hunt Morgan's Confederate Cavalry. The cavalry was captured during a later raid and sent to the Ohio Penitentiary to serve time. In Ohio, they were emphatically known as "Morgan's Raiders." These men were viewed as scoundrels and horse thieves, hence the prison sentence as opposed to time in a prisoner-of-war camp. In November 1863, Morgan and six of his officers escaped the prison by tunneling from their cells into the courtyard, where they scaled the prison walls and ran to freedom. Ohio was the farthest north any Confederate unit had ever made it into Union territory.

One thing I have always loved about my home state of Ohio is that its rich history. From the first settlers in the late 1700s to its role in the Civil War; from the eight United States Presidents born here to Thomas Edison and the Wright Brothers; from the first professional football team in Canton, Ohio, to the first professional baseball team in Cincinnati, Ohio; the state abounds with historical significance.

As Dodger and I walked south from Old Washington, we found another kind of history—a kind you can't find in a brochure or a history book. This is the silent history that has been left behind by the millions of settlers who tamed the Ohio wilderness. With it are more questions than answers. Here beside the road were four weathered gravestones standing solemnly inside a small, fenced-in cemetery. I read the faded names of John Ledman and his wife, Catherine, and their son and daughter. It appeared that John, who died in 1854, was a Revolutionary War veteran. Catherine died several years later at the age of 73. Both of their children were born in the 1790s and died in the 1880s. This little catacomb was all that remained of their lives. I wondered to myself: where was their house located? Where are their descendents today? Do their great-great grandchildren visit this site often? Do any Ledmans live near here? Did they achieve their dreams before they passed away? What *were* their dreams? I had much to ponder as I continued down that back road, so rich with the ghosts of Ohio's past.

~

Next morning the temperature was crisp, and I lay awake thinking back to the days I'd woken to the sound of an alarm clock. This morning was much different than those spent back at the factory. The pace had changed; I could awaken of my own volition—not the alarm clocks. Today I woke gently as the sun warmed my face. I peered down from my perch beside the fire tower at the foggy landscape of Seneca Lake below me. The birds sang and the sun worked hard to burn through the morning fog hovering on the lake below. As the fog thinned the lakes surface turned a dazzling red, reflecting the rays of the morning sun. Dodger and I lingered in silence, watching the show that Mother Nature was putting on for us. Finally we shouldered our packs just as the sun had climbed high enough to bring the fiery show to an end.

Our morning walk led us past the crash site and monument of the USS Shenandoah. On September 3, 1925, the dirigible exploded and crashed. The Shenandoah was a U.S. Navy airship and was built in Lakehurst, New Jersey, as a weapons system, flying laboratory and scouting vessel. It took sixteen months and a $1.5 million to build. When completed, the immense airship was 680 feet long and ninety-three feet high—that's over two football fields long and nine stories high! Its first flight was on September 4, 1923. Who would have dreamed then that just twenty-four months later, in a storm over southeastern Ohio, it would crash? The Shenandoah had completed fifty-eight flights, logging a total of 740 flight hours. The explosion and crash occurred during the Noble County Fair. Everyone there saw it, watching helplessly as the ship exploded, splitting into several sections and falling to the ground in a fiery crash. In a time when airplanes were an uncommon sight, this must have been horrifying. Fourteen crewmembers died that day, including the Captain, Lieutenant Commander Zachary Lansdowne. Interstate 77 covers much of the crash site today, although this and two other sites have been preserved.

On I hiked, daydreaming of the early days of aviation and remembering my time aboard the USS America where I worked as an aviation electrician's mate in the U.S. Navy. Lost in my thoughts paying little attention to my surroundings I nearly stepped on a bright yellow creature just off the trail. I stopped dead in my tracks. I had never seen such a creature.

"Dodger!" I shouted. "Hey, Dodger! You gotta come back here and see this thing!"

Dodger quickly returned, and we both realized it was a caterpillar. We marveled at the Jiminy Cricket–looking creature before us. Its head was much too big for its body, and it had a painted-on mustache, which made it look like a caricature of a French artist. Two huge black circles atop its head appeared to be eyes but were just markings to make the bug look more formidable to its opponents. I took several pictures of the fellow and later learned that it would someday be a tiger swallowtail butterfly.

The next morning was gray and dreary, and rain looked imminent. We followed the blue blazes of the Buckeye Trail south out of the town of Sharon, along County

Route 39. Just outside of town, when we were too far out to go back and seek refuge, the rain began to fall. We hiked all day through the soft and steady rain. We eventually turned on to Route 78, a busy road with trucks hauling coal and logs from the rich Ohio countryside. We passed another of the USS Shenandoah crash sites and stopped to enjoy lunch at a picnic table there.

We planned to camp in the Ohio Power Company's "Gamelands." The Ohio Power Company owns this strip-mined—and now reclaimed—land and maintains it as a wilderness area as a way for them to give back to the people from whom they have taken so much. Just short of our campsite, we met Jim Sprague, the former president of the Buckeye Trail Association. An older gentleman with a smile and a glow about him, he chatted with us about our journey and told us that the rest of his trail maintenance crew was camped near our campsite.

The rain had stopped by the time we reached the campsite, and we had little trouble picking out the maintenance crew. This was quite a group of trail maintainers: Herb Hulls the current Buckeye Trail president; Paul Daniels, the American Discovery Trail state coordinator; and Mike Minium, the U.S. Orienteering Federation's vice president. Along with Jim and another volunteer named Don, they were building a 100-foot-long footbridge across the bogs and marsh of the lowlands that lay just to the south. We enjoyed dinner with them as the rains returned. When the mosquitoes appeared, hungry for their dinner, we all headed to our tents.

I was nearly asleep when I heard someone calling my name from the darkness. It was Mike Schwager, my long-time friend and former co-worker from the Colgate factory in Cambridge Ohio. He had vowed to catch up with me while I was in the area. I was quite a ways from Cambridge now and had not expected to see him, but he kept his word. With him were his two daughters, Lauren and Lisa. We told a few stories and wished each other well, not knowing when we would meet again.

The next morning everything was soaked from the night's slow, steady rain. It made for a cool, misty morning—actually a great day for hiking, as it wouldn't be too hot. Toting our sopping-wet tents in our damp packs, Dodger and I headed out in search of the new footbridge. We descended the hill to the creek and marsh, where we found Herb and company putting the finishing touches on the handrail of a rustic log bridge. Dodger and I walked across the sturdy bridge, the first hikers to use this structure that will ease the trips of many hikers to come. We thanked the maintainers before moving on, continuing our hike along the Buckeye Trail.

Later that morning, Dodger slipped on some wet rocks on the trail. He fell hard, knocking the wind out of him. He rested a minute before removing his pack and climbing back to his feet.

"I'm OK," he hoarsely groaned, in answer to my un-asked question. I sat with him as he rested for about fifteen minutes. When we resumed hiking, Dodger walked a bit slower, wary of the slippery trail, the legacy of yesterday's rain. By afternoon we finished the wooded trail section and were now hiking on back roads again.

"Where're ya goin'?" We looked up to see a fellow on his porch who had spotted us.

"Louisiana!" we replied in unison. His jaw dropped, but he soon recovered and wished us luck. I'm sure he was wondering why anyone would set out to walk from Ohio to Louisiana.

Soon we neared a family picnic. Shortly after, we saw a man running from the picnic to the road.

"I'm Jim," he said, grinning. "Are you hungry?" His
wife, Angela, had seen us hiking and thought we might be
hungry, so he had come to invite us to his family reunion fish
fry. He'd caught all of the fish on one of his many fishing
excursions; certainly some had come from the Ohio Power
ponds we had passed earlier. We talked with Jim and his
wife before receiving a massive plate of deep-fried catfish
with all the fixings. While eating, we were surrounded by
the numerous children there who wanted to hear stories of
life on the trail. We willingly shared with them the joy we
found hiking the Appalachian Trail and now across Ohio. In
return, they told us of their school heroics and of life in
southeastern Ohio. When it came time to leave, we bid them
all a hearty thank-you and reluctantly shouldered our packs.
Several of the children asked if they could walk a ways with
us, as they lived just down the road. Their parents
consented, and the next half-mile was spent with an
entourage of local kids laughing and asking more questions.
It was quite a scene: two scruffy hikers with a group of
skipping, running, talkative children. When we reached their
houses they walked across their yards towards home.
Dodger and I walked on, waving and shouting back to them.
Soon it was quiet.

An hour or so later, we passed a run-down shanty
with a good ole boy standing in the open front door.

"Hey, ya thirsty?" he yelled up to the road. "I'm just
a hillbilly but I'd share a drink with you."

We stopped again, this time to meet JR. His house
was made from the scraps of houses that the local mining
companies had torn down. JR was proud of the place, even
though it was not yet finished. The bedroom was merely a
mattress on the floor, against the far wall, and the living
room was furnished with a chair and an old beaten couch.
The plywood floor had not been swept in some time and was

cluttered with tools and keepsakes. The kitchen had
beautiful cupboards; that seemed very out of place. It was
home though, and JR he was kind enough to invite us in to
enjoy a cold beer with him.

We ended our full day on the sleepy banks of the
Muskingum River, looking across it to Stockport, Ohio.
Long before airplanes or trains, water ruled; the waterways
are what connected the communities in southeast Ohio, as
well as the rest of the world. As the Ohio frontier—and later
the western edge of American expansion—began to develop,
travel by water was the quickest method available. The
problem was that many of the rivers in Ohio were not
reliable; they would dry up in the hot summers and were
deep and swift in the springtime, making them unsafe to
navigate.

The answer to this problem was the Ohio and Erie
Canal project, designed in the early 1820's to link Lake Erie
with the Ohio River and give the small towns along the route
access to the business world outside. Logically it would
have come along the Muskingum River through the
Stockport area, then south to Marietta. The fight for
inclusion on the route was intense, and in the end politics—
not logic—ruled. The canal, which was completed in 1832,
was routed farther west to Chillicothe, then the Ohio state
capital, and on south to Portsmouth.

In 1836, however, the Muskingum River valley was
finally developed when a series of locks and dams were
built, allowing year-round navigation of the entire river. A
person could boat from Zanesville all the way to Marietta
and the Ohio River. The cost of the project was $1.63
million, an astronomical amount for the time. The river
communities boomed, and industry grew up and down the
river. Competition from the trucking and rail industries,
along with major repair costs, brought the locks to a close in

1948. The entire system is still in place today, and the state of Ohio is currently looking at it as a potential recreational draw for the area. It is the only complete, hand-operated lock-and-dam system left intact in the nation.

The next day, I saw my first North Country Trail and American Discovery Trail markers. These two long trails are part of the National Trails System, and both pass through southern Ohio, following, for the most part, the Buckeye Trail Route. The North Country Trail is more than 4,000 miles long and stretches from the Finger Lakes region of New York west to North Dakota. The American Discovery Trail reaches from Delaware to San Francisco. Neither of these two trails is completely off-road, but both have completed routes that can be hiked in their entirety.

Labor Day came and went, and we continued our walk through Ohio. We hiked through the Trimble Wildlife Area, only to find a trash dump at a trail summit. It was disheartening. I felt like the American Indian in the "Keep America Beautiful" campaign of the early 1970s. He stands with a tear running down his cheek at the pain of seeing the utter disregard for our land that so many people have. A few days before that we had hiked around the Wolf Creek Wildlife Area. No roads pass through this area, and the Ohio Department of Natural Resources has decided not to allow a footpath to be built through it either. The reason? It would be disruptive to the wildlife. I'm confused with this policy. It's legal to trap, hunt, ride a four-wheeler, and evidently dump your trash in a wildlife area, but a footpath has been deemed too invasive? What a conundrum.

Later in the day, while taking a break along side a desolate dirt road, I noticed a bee that appeared to be stuck in a flower. I had never seen a bee stuck in a flower before, so I moved closer to get a better look. Sure enough, its pollen-gathering nose was stuck right in that flower. It was a buzzing as hard as it could but could not get out. I looked even closer to learn the source of the flower's grip: a tiny white spider. It had apparently lain in wait for something to come along, and this bee was the unlucky victim. When the bee landed, the spider attacked and held on with all its might. I watched for several minutes as the monumental struggle of life and death continued. Finally, the bee surrendered. The spider had won this battle against an insect at least five times its size.

Several days later, I called home to check in. I learned that my eight-year-old niece, Samantha, had broken her arm while doing cartwheels. Her arm was in a cast, but she would be fine. I realized that as I traverse along the back roads of southern Ohio, I sometimes forget that there is another world out there—the world I left behind. Often all that exists for me is my current space. My concentration is primarily on my next source of water and food.

~

Soon I found myself surrounded in the tranquility and beauty of Hocking Hills State Forest. I had first visited these hills when I was an eleven year old Boy Scout. The sandstone cliffs rise seventy to one hundred feet above the musky forest floor. The stream that runs through the ravine is a swirling cavalcade of water that flows and drops again and again through the gorge that is known as Hocking Hills.

Dodger was well ahead of me, and I walked these hills alone, but somehow I didn't feel alone. I stopped several times as wave after wave of emotion passed through me. Eventually I gave in to my emotion, and sat gazing distantly at the forest around me.

It was a dreary day, the sky dishwater gray. As I sat in the forest, I imagined I was in an abandoned old house,

littered with a world of ghosts and noises of the creatures
that make these woods their home. I was distinctly aware of
my visitor status in these woods. I listened for the skitterings
of creatures: a chipmunk, or mouse perhaps; but heard only
the sibilant breezes through the trees. The trees were mostly
young and thin-trunked, due to the history of logging in the
area. There were some old, gnarled ones still standing; their
branches were high, and their trunks thick with age. These
were the ghosts for me—the ancient inhabitants of this
abandoned old house of a forest. I thought about how these
woods must have looked three hundred years before, and
about the skeletons it had seen over the years—skeletons of
animals, skeletons of trees, skeletons of old roads, skeletons
of people—skeletons of dreams.

The Shawnee and Miami tribes once made their
home in these forests. Their skeletons and spirits haunt this
old house of logs, leaves, and dirt. Tecumseh, Chief Logan,
Blue Jacket, Cornstalk, Little Turtle, Black Fish, Black Hoof,
Pontiac, Tarhe, Simon Girty, and Daniel Boone have walked
among these hills. At the turn of the nineteenth century, as
more settlers streamed into Ohio, the Shawnee and Miami
people fought hard to keep this land. Tecumseh had a grand
plan of uniting all of the Native American tribes in the
untamed western country into a coalition to expunge the
Americans from the western lands forever. He traveled far
and wide, building a great coalition of over 3,000 natives.
At one point, warriors from the Wyandot, Mingo, Miami,
Kickapoo, Delaware, Shawnee, Ottawa, Ojibwe,
Potawatomi, Chickamauga, Fox, Sauk, and Mascouten were
in the alliance.

In the fall of 1811, Tecumseh went south to recruit
the Chickasaw, Choctaw, Creek, and Cherokee into the
alliance. He left his brother, The Prophet, in charge in Ohio,
giving him specific instructions to avoid a confrontation with

the Americans. William Henry Harrison, later to become President of the U.S., was responsible for settling the Ohio frontier. Playing on The Prophet's personal greed for fame and recognition, Harrison tricked Tecumseh's brother into engaging in battle while Tecumseh was away. The Indians were soundly defeated, and Tecumseh's years of effort were quickly undone. The thousands of Indians who had gathered in western Ohio and Indiana dispersed back to their own villages, dejected and worried about the imminent struggle that lay ahead for their own lands. Tecumseh's dream for a native coalition died with him during the war of 1812, when he was killed in Canada at the Battle of Thames. His burial place is unknown.

As I sat in deep thought, nearly overwhelmed with all that ran through my mind, I wrote my thoughts down, and in the end came up with a poem.

As we cut into Mother Earth
To rob her heart,
Oh, my friend, I hear you cry,
And to this day I wonder why
The words you spoke we could not hear.
All I can do, my friend, is add a tear.

We didn't understand then your wisdom and
foresight,
So now we dwell in our own refuse.
We wrote down your words and still preach them
today
But we have yet to hear what you had to say.
Oh, where are the bear, the buffalo, the wapiti?
We have traded them to make room for hay
And now the silence of your forest

Is disrupted by the trucks that haul Mother Earth
away.

A tree will lean to get to the light
Nature is that way
But what will the tree do when there is no more light?

How many more mountaintops will we blow up
To make room for another ski resort?
How many more marshes will we drain and fill
To make room for another Wal-Mart?

Oh, Tecumseh, will we ever listen to your words
And comprehend your wisdom?
Or will we just add a tear?

~

That September of 2001 Ohio continued to suffer from a serious drought. The waterfalls and swirls had been reduced to a mere trickle. Ironically, water damage from a flood several years before is the reason for the massive construction project that took place in the gorge as we hiked through. The area is very heavily visited, so the forest service is putting in sidewalks to make the area handicapped-accessible as well as to limit the damage done by the masses of people who come to see the beauty of Hocking Hills. We passed through quietly, the only visitors with backpacks on, and soon we were again on the back roads that had become our home.

We later reached the weathered Grove Hopewell Church. Like many of the churches we passed in southern Ohio, Grove Hopewell was built long before plumbing was common and still operates today with no plumbing. Each church generally has an outhouse—a true blessing for a passing hiker! The outhouses are labeled in many odd ways, denoting one for men and another for women. The local folks generally don't have a hard time spelling *men*, but *women* seems to hold a greater challenge. I have seen them labeled as "wemem" and "wimem," as well as other misspellings I don't recall. Time has passed very slowly here, and in many ways it seems Grove Hopewell hasn't reached the twenty-first century.

As Dodger and I pitched our tents in the churchyard, a pickup truck pulled in. It was the Pastor, Tommy. He was a young man who had not been ordained, but volunteered to lead the church. His grandparents had attended here, as had he as a child. His children were now the fourth generation in his family to grace the pews of this small country chapel. He stopped to see what we were doing and make sure we did not need anything. Of course we were fine, and enjoyed the pleasant visit with Tommy.

Several mornings later, I hiked through a scenic little valley nestled in the rural farming community near Eagle Mills, Ohio. The road seemed deserted with a few scattered houses dotting the landscape, most of them in need of repair. I started across a bridge with Salt Creek beneath me. I looked up to see a man walking towards me. His clothes were rumpled, and his hair was uncombed. I smiled thinking that he looked a lot like me. We met in the middle of the bridge.

"What're ya doin' out here?" he quickly asked me, and I proceeded to tell him about the hike to see America. I can be a bit long-winded, and I noticed as I talked that he was antsy to speak. I finally finished, and he asked enthusiastically, "Do ya need a bath?"

Well, *this* took me by surprise I thought my spiel about my hike would surprise *him*.

"Pardon me?" I replied, wanting to make sure I had heard him correctly.

He nearly cut me off as he continued. "I reckon with ya walkin' all over the country, ya don't get to get cleaned up very often! Do ya need to get a bath?"

"Um … I guess …" I stood there, thinking he wanted to invite me home but then he turned toward the creek below us and pointed downstream.

"See that deep spot down there? That's whar I get *mah* bath." He grinned at me, then turned again, this time pointing to the bank. "And there on the bank, ya see that downed tree?"

I nodded, peering.

"Well, thar's a flat spot on the top of it. That's whar I keep m'soap. Feel free to use it if ya need to."

Unable to say much more, I thanked him for the offer, and we each went our separate ways. I didn't realize we still had people bathing in the streams of America, let alone in the supposedly industrialized and developed state of Ohio, not far from my own backyard!

On September 9, 2001 my time on the Buckeye Trail would come to an end. My route would take me south to Portsmouth, while the Buckeye Trail continues westward towards Chillicothe. The Buckeye Trail is truly a treasure for the citizens of Ohio and all those who come to hike it. Someday I hope to do the rest, but for now, Kentucky beckoned.

The seasons were beginning to change as I neared the end of my Ohio journey. The farmers' fields were filled with dying crops of yellow, green, and brown. The roadsides were dappled orange, purple, and yellow with late summer wildflowers. We walked among hills that jutted up some two to three hundred feet around us.

One afternoon, Dodger and I stopped to chat with a worn old farmer, his face weathered from too many years in the sun. I don't recall the entire conversation, but as we parted he said, "When you get to be my age, every day is a blessing."

As we walked off, 54-year-old Dodger looked at me and asked, "Why do people have to grow old to figure that out?"

We camped that night along the banks of the Scioto River. The fish were jumping, eating the bugs that hovered just above the water. A few boats came trolling by in hopes of catching a bass or a crappie. As the darkness fell, I watched a muskrat swimming silently up the river. There was harmony in this world, and calmness ruled as the sun set.

The goal for our last day in Ohio was to hike thirteen miles to the town of Portsmouth. We got an early start that morning; we wanted to have plenty of time to accomplish our town chores such as laundry and grocery shopping. My radio, fondly named Coby, was playing classical music as we hiked along. Shortly after nine, the music was interrupted by a news brief. It was the beginning of that horrific day, September 11, 2001. Dodger was ahead of me, and I hollered for him to wait. We listened together as the second plane crashed into the World Trade Center. In utter disbelief, we continued our journey to Portsmouth. A few cars pulled over to ask if we had heard the news. All faces were stricken, as I'm sure ours were as well. We reached town in the early afternoon, got a hotel room, and remained glued to the news channels the rest of the day.

The mood of our hike had suddenly changed, and I questioned whether my great adventure should continue. Did my country need me elsewhere now? I had served in the Navy, and I thought of visiting the local recruiter to see if I was needed for service again. I decided to wait a while and see if a call came for veterans to serve again.

Taking the next day off, I decided to stop at the local American Legion. It was good to be around other veterans and, while the current attacks controlled much of our discussion early on, we also talked about Portsmouth and its unique history. The men talked proudly of days past when Portsmouth had its own NFL team, the Portsmouth Spartans. The Spartans were in Portsmouth from 1930 until 1934. In 1931, their 11-3 record was good enough for second place. The Green Bay Packers won their third title in a row by finishing 12-2 that year, and they refused to play the Spartans in a championship game. The next season, with a record of 6-1-4, the Spartans finished in a tie for the NFL title with the Chicago Bears. For the first time, two teams finished tied atop the league's standings. The league office arranged for the first playoff game in NFL history. The game was moved indoors to Chicago Stadium because of bitter cold and heavy snow. The arena was small and had only enough room for an eighty-yard field. The field came right to the walls and the goal posts were moved from the end lines to the goal lines. The Bears won that day, 9-0, scoring the winning touchdown on a two-yard pass from Bronko Nagurski to Red Grange. The game would lead to divisional play and an annual playoff game to decide the NFL Championship in future years.

In 1933, the Spartans struggled all season to finish with a disappointing 6-5 record. It would turn out to be their final season in the small town of Portsmouth, Ohio. The NFL was moving into larger cities, and the Spartans moved to Detroit where they established a new tradition as the Lions. My new friends at the American Legion also told me of Branch Rickey, who was born in Portsmouth. He was the General Manager of the Brooklyn Dodgers who signed

Jackie Robinson, breaking the color barrier in professional sports.

It was an educational afternoon, and the talk of football helped me to focus on something other than the tumultuous world around me. Dodger and I discussed whether we should continue with the hike, or if we stop here due to the inevitable war the country would soon be in. After discussing the matter with family and friends, we decided that the hike is what we could give our country for now. I hoped that, through my online journal, I could provide something positive to others—something to let them know America is still a safe place. A way to bring some good news into their lives.

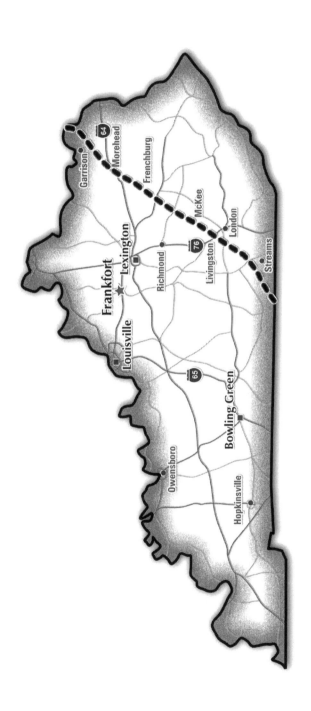

Kentucky

It was early October, 1789. Her husband Thomas was in town, selling the crops the family had spent all summer growing. Jenny watched helplessly as the Indian savages, painted for war, killed her three oldest children and fifteen-year-old brother. Soon the Indians disappeared into the forest from where they came, taking with them a pregnant Jenny and her infant son. Several days later, she watched helplessly as her child was taken from her and bashed against a tree, killed for crying, killed to keep the settlers in hot pursuit off their trail.

She and her captors walked for several days before they forded the Big Sandy River, an arduous task normally, made more difficult with pregnancy. Several days later, they reached the Ohio River and saw the Shawnee town on the other side, in the area that is now Portsmouth. Heavy rains had flooded the river, and crossing the mighty Ohio was not an option. They set up camp and settled for the winter in Kentucky.

One night the Indians brought a captured white man into camp, and Jenny watched as they tortured him and burned him at the stake. Later that night, they told her that she, too, would soon suffer the same fate. A few days later, when the camp was almost empty, she saw her chance and ran into the forest, literally running for her life. Miraculously, she found her way and made it to safety after several days on the run.

Jenny Wiley was eventually reunited with her husband, with whom she had six more children. She died in 1831 at the age of 71, and is buried near the Jenny Wiley State Resort Park in Prestonburg Kentucky. . Our next trail was the Jenny Wiley Trail, which runs from Portsmouth to the Kentucky state park named in her honor.

Still in shock from the terrorist attacks, I caught the news one last time as I hoisted my pack which was laden with four days' worth of food. It was time to head south. Dodger and I walked through town along the floodwall, which was painted as a continuous history mural. It is almost a quarter of a mile long and depicts the rich history of this small river town. We reached the bridge and began to cross the Ohio River. Just downstream is where the Scioto River empties into the Ohio. This was where the Shawnee had brought Jenny Wiley so many years ago.

As we reached the Kentucky shore, a Kentucky state policeman greeted us. He had received several calls about two strangers walking on the bridge. I guess fear of further attacks had people worried. We spoke with the officer, telling him of our great adventure, and then we asked him to help us find the Jenny Wiley Trail, which was supposed to start right across the river. He gave us a free county map and pointed us in the right direction.

We soon found the trailhead and started down the Jenny Wiley Trail. It was easy hiking the rolling Kentucky hills for the first six miles. Then after a road crossing, the trail started up a small hill, and the nicely worn trail slowly disappeared into a thicket of multi-flora rose. The forest was much different when Jenny Wiley had made her escape, as it was then a virgin forest, having never been logged, or overrun by non-native species such as multi-flora rose. We tried to work our way around the overgrown section, but it was like walking through a prison fence. I felt like I was donating blood as my bare legs received slash after slash from the sharp thorns of the out-of-control underbrush. Where my legs did not bleed they stung from the nettles and thorns that were like tiny hairs of poison being imbedded into my skin.

Dodger and I painfully retreated to the road, unsure of which way to turn. We headed west and several miles later arrived at a main road.

We stopped at a local store where we were greeted by Sierra Layne, a talkative, joyful middle-aged woman behind the counter. We learned that we were about two miles from where we had crossed the bridge into Kentucky. We had just spent most of the day covering two measly miles.

We decided to get a bite to eat. Sierra, very excited about our journey, asked question after question as she prepared our meal. As we ate, she greeted each new customer, making sure to tell each one about our grand adventure.

"Hey there! Have you got any idea what these two men are a doin'? Well, let me tell ya. They just walked here from Ohio and are hiking all across the country. Ain't that somethin'?"

Most of the customers stopped at our table to chat and wish us well. We asked for more information on the Jenny Wiley Trail, hoping to find our route again. We were strongly advised to avoid the northern section of it, as it had fallen into disrepair, and it was just like the overgrown gauntlet of thorns we had just encountered. We decided to hike the railroad tracks south to Vanceburg instead. One of the two sets of tracks had been removed, making the walk much more tolerable.

Dodger and I managed to hike a few more miles before finding a sandy campsite along the banks of the still industrially important Ohio River. We pitched our tents and cooked dinner, waving to passing boaters and watching the tugboats push the barges up and down the busy river. The sunset was spectacular, glimmering off the still, deep waters of the mighty river, the green hills of Ohio casting long shadows back at us as the sun slowly retreated behind them.

A few days later, we found ourselves sitting at the entrance to Daniel Boone National Forest, having hiked the back roads from our river campsite through the Kentucky hills, passing tobacco barn after tobacco barn. I found it odd that there were no tobacco barns in Ohio; surely the soil was not that much different. The difference was the river. That was the dividing line between North and South. In the South, tobacco rules. The brown and yellow leaves hung inside the specially designed barns in almost every yard we passed. The barns themselves had hundreds of little shutters running down the sides to allow air to pass through and assist in the drying of the tobacco leaves. Inside them hung row after row of this year's crop. In many of the fields, the tobacco had been cut and bound, making little pyramids neatly placed, waiting their turn in the barn. Some fields were still planted, waiting their turn to be harvested. I was certainly in the South now.

~

On September 15, 2001 we reached the Daniel Boone National Forest and began hiking on the Sheltowee Trace National Recreation Trail. It felt good to be back on a footpath again and off the roads. The shade of the trees and the sounds of the birds chirping was much more relaxing than the rumbling of cars passing by, each one in a hurry to get somewhere. We had planned to camp at a Forest Service campground, but the side trail which was clearly marked on our forest service maps, had thus-far eluded us. Dodger hiked ahead, and I expected to find him sitting at the trail junction waiting for me. Much to my surprise, I found him walking back towards me, with a woman at his side.

He had met Jennifer, who was out for a day hike. She soon led us to the trail we had somehow both passed up. We backtracked a quarter mile or so and learned that Jennifer was the head softball coach at Morehead State University in nearby Morehead, Kentucky. The three of us hiked down off the hill, along the unmarked trail. The path ended at a road that led through a nice neighborhood; and the National Forest Campground was at the far end of the development.

Jennifer invited us in for a shower and to enjoy a soft drink with her and her roommate. I learned that Jennifer had been to my high school in Wintersville, Ohio, recruiting softball players. I asked her where she was from and she replied "Louisa, Kentucky." I shook my head in disbelief. I had been to the small Kentucky town of Louisa. I dated Amy Wallace from Louisa back in 1983 when we both worked at Camp Sequoia in the Catskill Mountains of New York. We planned to hike around Europe together that fall, but I shelved the plans and joined the Navy instead. Amy ended up going to Europe alone and never forgave me. Jennifer had gone to the same high school as Amy and knew her. What a small world. Refreshed by the shower and giddy over my chance meeting with Jennifer, I walked with Dodger down to the campground. It was already nine-thirty and neither of us felt much like pitching a tent, so we slept on picnic tables in the pavilion.

The next morning, Dodger and I hiked into the town of Morehead. I had a pair of long pants mailed to me here, to help me make it through the overgrown sections of trail. The town is large and finding the post office proved to be a chore, but after an hour or so of hiking around town and asking directions we made it. My package was not there.

We decided to stay a day and to see if it would make it into town.

We got a hotel room for the night and showered for the second day in a row before finding a place to enjoy dinner. Our waitress was a high school student named Kasie Walling. She was very interested in our journey, and we chatted with her for some time. Her other tables did not receive the same level of service as ours, as she repeatedly came by to make sure we had enough tea and hear more of our story. Little did I know then the impact I would have on Kasie—or the impact she would have on me.

Back at the post office, I hoped my mail would be there. I waited the customary ten minutes in line before my turn arrived. I walked to the counter and asked if there might be a General Delivery Package for Dan Rogers. The clerk looked at me like I was from another planet.

"General Delivery," she asked. I explained my journey to her and that General Delivery service was one that I used frequently. She went in the back and looked, but found no mail for me again today. I could not take another day off, so I asked her if I could forward the package to another location along the trail. On the Appalachian Trail this was no problem. The post offices deal with hikers and General Delivery on a daily basis. In Morehead, Kentucky, however, General Delivery was as foreign as I myself with my backpack and carefree demeanor.

The postal clerk informed me that I would need to set up a General Delivery account before she could forward anything, and handed me a form. I asked her politely for the form that would simply allow me to forward any mail I might get; I did not want to set up an account with them. She insisted she was right, so I got out of line to fill out the form.

Again I waited the customary ten minutes to return to the front of the line. This time I walked to the other clerk, explained my situation, then handed her my completed form. She looked at the form, then looked at me and said, "Oh my, you don't need this form. You need the forwarding form." My first reaction was one of frustration. I knew that is what I needed; I had asked for that form. I began to raise my voice at her, but I caught myself and thanked her. I quickly filled out the form while standing in line. I knew she had just saved me a lot of headache later on. Hopefully someday, I would see my mail.

Hiking that afternoon, I heard so few birds. I noticed that the forest was very young and wondered if the trees perhaps were not mature enough to bear fruit. I thought if this were true, perhaps that would explain the lack of wildlife in this area—no food, no animals. The logging activity that had occurred here twenty years or so before still affects the land today. Mother Nature does heal, but always at her own pace. At times, that pace can be very slow.

The afternoon was beautiful with a slight breeze. I crested the hill and saw Dodger one hundred yards ahead of me, standing in the middle of the trail. . . with a horse. He had been talking of getting a pet lately, but this was ridiculous.

"Where did you find this pet?" I exclaimed.

Dodger replied, "Can I *keep* her?"

"I told you no pets! What are we going to do with a horse?"

The full-grown chestnut brown horse was obviously lost and had countless burrs in her mane and tail. Our presence had excited her, and she was prancing around. She certainly seemed to like Dodger, following him and as he headed down the trail. She liked him so much that she refused to let me pass her; no way were we leaving her behind. We continued down the trail: Dodger, the horse, and me. We decided to name her "Old Paint." When Dodger slowed down or stopped to talk, she would nudge him in the back, as if to say "Keep it moving up there! I am getting out of here today!" After about a mile, we reached a huge tree that had fallen across the trail. Dodger and I were able to go under it. Old Paint quickly ran around, and forced her way back in line, taking her place in our little procession again.

Several miles later, we reached a road crossing. Old Paint was now distraught, afraid of passing cars. She ran back into the woods fifty yards or so. I looked across the road and saw an empty, fenced-in pasture with a small stream running through the middle of it. It seemed to call to us, "Hey—hey you—yeah, you with the horse—put the horse in here." There were no other animals in it so Dodger and I decided the pasture would be her home, at least for now.

Dodger went to the house nearby to ask permission while I tried to get the horse across the road safely. I had no luck, as each time she seemed ready, a car came by and scared her back up the hill. Dodger returned to inform me that the folks in the house merely rented; they did not own the pasture. A Forest Service employee came by and we explained our dilemma to him. He thought we were doing the right thing but offered no help. He watched as we were able to calm her and coax her across the road. I held the gate open and she ran inside, bucking and galloping as if in celebration. She ran large circles around the pasture, enjoying her new home.

We walked back to the house to let the renters know they had inherited a horse. They agreed to call the owner and the local police to see if a missing horse had been reported. As we hiked on past Old Paint, she was prancing, enjoying the wide-open space of the manicured pasture. The green grass was thick, and she was partaking freely of the feast. We passed out of sight, knowing we had done the best we could.

A few miles later, we reached a small, rundown country store where we found several older gentlemen sitting on the porch, sharing lies and laughing. We decided to join them for a bit. We were immediately welcomed and joined in the conversation, which quickly turned to tales of our adventure. It was here that I discovered the drink called Ale 8 One, pronounced "A Late One" It is a local Kentucky beverage that is very heavy in ginger—definitely a different kind of soft drink. I wondered why we hadn't gotten this across the river. We chatted with the locals for an hour or so before heading back to the forest to camp for the night.

Kentucky is a beautiful state, and its hills are splendid. The area is filled with deep hollows and scenic bluffs. Oak, hickory and pine dominate the ridges while the cool, moist gorges are populated with hemlock, yellow poplar, sugar maple, sycamore, and beech trees. Through time the wind and water have created more than eighty arches in the soft sandstone cliffs there.

The morning's hike led us to the Clifty Wilderness area of Daniel Boone National Forest. We entered and descended gradually along an old roadbed for several miles. Once in the gorge, we hiked along the Red River for several more miles, enjoying its uncomplicated beauty. The water, crisp and clear, flowed effortlessly onward. The path here was narrow and the weeds and bushes were covered with yesterday's rain. I felt the cool droplets of water brushing against my legs and arms as I hiked, cooling my skin even as the day warmed up. We passed several rock outcroppings, that loomed five hundred feet or so overhead. I noticed stands of rhododendron and mountain laurel in abundance. We crossed the stream several times, getting our socks and shoes wet with each crossing. With our shoes saturated, we left the stream and valley, climbing to the ridgeline, crossing into the Red River Gorge Wilderness area of the forest.

My spirit soared on the ridgeline. I hiked among the tall trees while puffy white clouds danced in the sky. My shoes slowly dried, and my feet rejoiced at the thought of also being dry again. After several miles my shoes were finally dry enough to put on my fresh socks. As I was changing socks I noticed a hole in the heel of one of the socks I had just taken off.

We arrived at camp about 5:15 to find the park closed, presumably for the season. Having hiked twenty-one miles already, we decided to stay anyhow. We pitched our tents in the quietness of the empty campground. It felt eerie to be there alone. It was much too early in September for the campground to be closed—but it was.

I had been here before on a weekend trip and remembered that there was a store about a mile and a half down the road. We needed some groceries, so off we went, on a three-mile bonus hike to get supplies.

On the way, we found Miguel's Pizza and Rock Climbing Store. We devoured a large pizza and talked with the crew there. As we prepared to leave, I noticed they sold wool socks. I certainly had not expected to replace my worn socks so quickly. It is odd the way the things we really need are somehow provided for us.

We walked down to the Daniel Boone Trading Post, a touristy little store with some basic camping food. We re-supplied there and tried to find a shirt or patch, anything with "Sheltowee" on it. I was humbled to find out that the folks running a store called the Daniel Boone Trading Post had never heard of the Sheltowee Trace Trail and didn't have a clue who or what the word *Sheltowee* meant. I guess that is the way tourism works. You sell what brings a quick easy buck, with little regard to the history and reality of your namesake. We made it back to the campground as God was turning the dark on. We sat up laughing and chatting for an hour or so before retiring for the night.

We were packing up our gear the next morning when the campground administrator arrived, followed closely by the work party. Dodger and I continued packing as we watched three men climb out of a state truck. They armed themselves with gas-powered blowers, ready to do battle with Mother Nature. They proceeded to blow the leaves from the road, the paths to the campsites.Finally they blew off the campsites. The thought of having leaves on the ground in the campsite area must have been too much to bear, as they were meticulous in their manner, blowing each leaf until the campsite was devoid of any sign that fall was coming and Mother Nature was at work. In their efforts, they created such a loud noise that they had to wear hearing protection. They probably scared every living thing within a half-mile. The gas-powered blowers spewed out smoke, polluting the air—all in the name of forest management.

It made for a great morning laugh and a topic of conversation for several days. I do hope my state taxes in Ohio are going for better things than this. The park host approached us, curious as to where our car was parked. We explained about the hike across America. She seemed like a wonderful lady and was reluctant to charge us, but not being paid to make decisions, only to follow tightly written guidelines, she did.

We hiked across the leaf-free pavement and out of the park, down to the Natural Bridge area where the trail split in two, with both routes leading to the Natural Bridge. One route led through a small cave while the other did not. I wanted to go through the cave, so Dodger consented. The cave was only about a quarter mile long and was an easy walk for most of the way. With our headlamps to light our way, we walked through until we could see the light at the other end. Soon after, the cave got smaller and smaller, squeezing us in until there was barely room for a man, let alone a man with a backpack on. I took my pack off while Dodger cussed up a storm behind me. He was not happy when I informed him we would have to crawl through.

"Dammit! I don't like this one bit. I don't like little spaces. You didn't tell me it would be this little. I am old. I can't be crawling all over the place. I am gonna get my pack dirty." His voice grew fainter as I squeezed through the small opening and into the open air above.

I laughed and yelled back down into the hole in the ground "Ahh come on ya old fart, get that pack off and squeeze through. It ain't that bad—I made it."

Dodger came through but was visibly shaken.

"I get claustrophobic. Damn, that was not fun."

He had never told me that before, and my continued laughter probably didn't make him feel any better. We continued on to the Natural Bridge, stopping to admire the mammoth arch that stood before us. The brown arch of sandstone loomed high above us, sitting alone in the middle of the forest.

We hiked under the arch, then up the narrow steps which were cut into the backside of the sandstone monolith, before emerging on top. On top we were treated with a magnificent view of the surrounding hills: the hills to the north that we had just traversed, and the hills to the south that lay ahead of us. We chatted with the many tourists up there before continuing south alone, away from the parking lot where the tourists would all retreat to. The concept of not having a car to return to was intriguing to them and I am sure they pondered our sanity as they retreated to the safety and comfort of their vehicles and hotel rooms.

A few days and several miles later, we entered a
beautiful area that was aptly named Sinking Creek. The
stream appeared and then disappeared under the rocks, only
to reappear again several hundred yards later. I heard the
water flowing beneath me as I rock-hopped across the
boulders that concealed the stream. The trail was very
confusing; this was four-wheeler country, and the trails of
the local riders went every which way, making it nearly
impossible to follow the sparsely blazed hiking trail. We
pushed onward, using the sun as our compass, hoping that
we would pop out of the forest where we were supposed to.
We didn't.

We did however finally reach a paved road several
miles from the trail. Here we sat with our maps, trying to
figure out the best way to get back onto the trail. We set out
across a small county road in search of our lost trail, and met
the Mays brothers and their family. They were sitting in
their front yard enjoying a Saturday afternoon beer.

In the group was Randy, his wife Pepper and their
three children: Jenny, Randy Jr., and Makala, who was three;
Randy's brother Buddy, his cousins Scottie and Curtis, and
some other friends had joined them as well. They were all
curious about our hike and asked us to chat with them for a
while. Deciding a short break would not hurt Dodger and I
walked up to the house. Dodger was soon telling the guys
about the journey while I became overrun with kids. The
three of them had obviously warmed up to me very quickly.
Makala, age three, had been playing in the dirt, making mud
pies. She came to me with a big white smile shimmering
between her dirty little cheeks and with a mud pie made just
for me. Soon I was leading the kids in silly songs I had
learned in the Boy Scouts and telling knock-knock jokes.
We made necklaces from fishing line and loose sandstone

rocks from the yard. The kids enjoyed the attention and we had a grand time.

Randy and his family lived in a trailer next door, while Buddy and Scottie lived in the house. Down back was a hen house with fifteen to twenty chickens running around. Sunk into the front yard was a small cement bathtub from before the days of indoor plumbing. I had never seen one before. It was no longer used for bathing, but had been reduced in importance to a place to throw empty beer cans until it was time to take them to the recycler.

None of adults had steady work—they did odd jobs to make ends meet. They were good people and we enjoyed their company. They invited us to have dinner and spend the night. We accepted and were treated to homemade cornbread, bean soup, and ham sandwiches. We sat up telling stories until about ten-thirty. As time for sleep came near, Dodger told me to take the spare bedroom, and that he would sleep in the backyard.

All was well until about three a.m. when I awoke to the sound of gunfire. I sat up and listened and soon realized that it was two-way gunfire. The house was being shot at! Completely confused, I ducked under my covers as if the thin layers of cotton would protect me. The shooting continued for about ten seconds, followed by a quiet stillness that was almost deafening. My heart raced...I could hear every beat pound in my brain. A million bad movies ran through my brain. I sat motionless for nearly fifteen minutes before gathering enough courage to walk out and see what had happened. Not knowing what to expect, I reached the corner of the hallway and peeked into the living room. I could see Buddy, shotgun in hand, still peering out the living room window.

"Hey—hey it's just me," I said softly.

With a hearty laugh, Buddy turned and replied, "Ahh man. I bet I scared you half to death. Man, I'm sorry!" Then, with a renewed laughter, he exclaimed, "I bet your buddy in the back is really shook!"

"Yeah, I bet he is," I murmured.

Buddy broke in again apologizing, "I certainly didn't expect all of this. Ya see, there's this old boy down the way; he has been giving us trouble for months. He pulled up in the yard and started cussin' at me." Buddy grinned. "I peppered his ass all the way home!"

I was relieved to know there were no casualties and sat down in the chair to regain my thoughts. In the distant night air, I could hear the siren. Shortly thereafter, I saw the flashing lights as the deputy sheriff of Lee County pulled into the drive. Thoughts of a damp Kentucky county jail raced through my mind as he stepped from his car. He took two steps and stopped. Buddy made no effort to hide his shotgun, which was now lying on the couch beside him.

The deputy yelled into the house, "Now, damn you boys! I told ya, ya have to keep it quiet out here. Ya hear me? I know you're in there! Ya just can't go shootin at all times of the night. This is a residential area, you got that? I had better not have to come back out here tonight."

With his speech delivered, the deputy stepped back into his car and was gone. I guess he could say he had responded to the call. Buddy again laughingly apologized as I went back to bed, hoping for a few more quiet hours of sleep. I finally drifted off.

At first light, Dodger was at the bedroom window knocking and whispering. "Sheltowee ... You in there? Hey, Sheltowee."

"I hear ya, I hear ya. Gimme a second."

"Hey, let's get moving."

I wearily got up and quietly packed my backpack.
Buddy was asleep on the couch as I headed out. He awoke
as I clamored through the house, my pack making it
impossible for me to walk quietly.

"Hey, y'all off already?" he asked in a sleepy
southern drawl.

"Didn't get near enough miles in yesterday, have to
make up for it today," I replied.

Dodger and I shook his hand and headed out the
door. As I walked out I looked across the yard at Randy's
trailer. In the bedroom window facing me was Jenny, saying
goodbye and waving. I hiked on, wondering if she would
grow up to graduate from high school. Wondering what the
future held for her.

We descended the ridge into the town of Heidelberg,
sitting on the banks of the Kentucky River. We stopped at
the lock and dam for lunch and soon we were back on the
Sheltowee Trace Trail. Late that afternoon, I met an elderly
woman sitting on her front porch. I looked up at her and
asked if I might be able to get some water from an outside
spigot. She smiled at me, said "certainly," and walked off
the porch, leading us around to the well behind the house.
She proceeded to drop the old wooden bucket down into the
well before slowly cranking it back up with the weathered
old hand crank. When it reached the top, she reached over
and grabbed an old, long-handled, tin drinking ladle. I
smiled as I stepped back in time. The water was so pure and
sweet as I drank from the ladle. I passed it to Dodger and
then we filled our bottles from the bucket. The three is us
talked of simpler times. As Dodger and I headed down the
road I had a strong feeling of peace—a feeling that this was
where I belonged.

It had been eight days and 145 miles since my last
shower. My body smelled, as did both pairs of my socks,

which had been worn four days each. My shirt was stained with the salt I had sweated out each day. I was ready for a shower, ready for clean clothes, and ready for a comfortable bed for the night. The weather was quickly turning colder and it was forecast to rain. We pushed hard, trying to make it to Interstate 75 and a hotel. We arrived at dusk to find only a truck stop. No motel. The weather deteriorated as we walked into the restaurant to formulate a plan. It felt good to be out of the cold wind, and in the warmth of the restaurant.

I inquired where the nearest hotel might be and was told it was nine miles down the interstate. I grabbed a phone book and called the only cab company listed—and got their answering machine. I left the message but had no clue if they would come and get us.

We ordered dinner, and then Dodger went on a recon mission to find a place to pitch our tents should the cab not come through. He soon returned with a chill, as the wind was blowing harder and colder. After finishing dinner, I again called the cab company, this time getting an answer. They would pick us up at nine-thirty. We reached town around ten and each enjoyed a good shower, one of life's simple pleasures. Those who shower every day surely cannot enjoy the true bliss of a good, hot shower after several days of hiking.

It was now late September. The weather remained cold for several days. The trail took us through the heart of the southern section of Daniel Boone National Forest, passing through several small mountain towns where we stopped for re-supply. Every town had at least one church with a cemetery. One day we stopped at the Pine Creek Church to enjoy lunch at the adjacent picnic shelter. Dodger decided to take a walk through the cemetery.

"Sheltowee, you need to come here," he called out a few minutes later.

The cemetery had a row of around thirty new graves marking unnamed infants. A fresh flower was planted at each grave. It was a place filled with broken dreams as well as dreams fulfilled. It was a very humble place, to say the least. A place that makes a man appreciate all he has—even when all he has is on his back.

A few days later, Dodger and I sat on a large rock next to the Cumberland River and watched the moon rise over the mountain behind us. As the moon climbed higher into the night sky, the mountain opposite from us slowly lit up. Soon, a small part of the white sand shoreline of the river was white again, while the rest of the shoreline was still black. We watched as the moon slowly rose and gave light to the nighttime. Owls hooted in the distance, and a muskrat swam across the river to his night-shift work. The trees now appeared as individuals, each with its own silhouette. Each tree, each branch, stood out against the brilliant moonlit sky. They were the kings of this forest as they swayed back and forth in the gentle nighttime breeze, each a part of the forest community, but each an individual tonight.

I awoke to the sound of a foghorn. Dodger was off first, and I followed fifteen minutes later. The landscape was diverse, from the deep green Cumberland River and her rapids and boulders on my right; to the mountainside at my left, with its high cliffs and nooks and caves; to the wide variety of plant life that was all around. We met a small group of backpackers, the first we had met on the Sheltowee Trace Trail. We also met a family on vacation from Indiana. They asked us if we were going to stay tonight at the falls to see the moonbow.

We had never heard of a moonbow, so it was an easy decision to stay in the park for the opportunity to see something so rare. We thanked the family and hiked into Cumberland Falls State Park. Here we looked at Cumberland

Falls, reputed to be the largest falls east of the Mississippi and south of Niagara Falls. They were indeed impressive. We left the falls area and walked up the hill to the campground. To our joy, we found a small store onsite with groceries suitable for backpacking. We showered, got all gussied up in our finest hiker attire, and went to dinner at the main lodge. We were treated to an incredible all-you-can-eat smorgasbord while we waited for the moonbow.

What is a moonbow, you ask. Moonbows only occur, on a regular basis, in two places on earth: here in Kentucky, and at Victoria Falls, in East Africa. The moon has to be at the full phase and the sky must be clear. The light of the moon, shining down on the waterfall will create a "rainbow" that begins at the base of the falls and projects down the river. On a perfect night, it will include the full spectrum of the rainbow, but a solid white bow is more common.

After dinner we made our way back to the falls. We were not disappointed in the show put on by Mother Nature. I gazed at the solid white arc of light that emanated from the base of the falls. I smiled deeply at the gift I had been given.

The next day, we had a leisurely morning of chores and packing. Coffee in the morning is one of life's little pleasures that I miss when hiking, so I was elated when our tent site neighbors, Bill and Phyllis, introduced themselves and offered to share their coffee with me.

I also had hoped to wash my socks this morning. The little store at Cumberland Falls State park, the only store around, was not open this morning. I would not be able to make change and I had only enough change for the dryer. I washed my socks by hand in the sink. After the chores were done, we pressed on. I had decided to save my coins and hung my wet pair of socks on my pack. We walked down to the waterfall and then south along the Sheltowee Trace Trail.

The river, now in a much wider gorge than on the other side of the waterfalls, was so peaceful to hike along. I jumped several ducks from the riverbank and saw a blue heron. After hiking about three miles, I met a family from Bowling Green, Kentucky, on a picnic. We chatted for some time and they offered me some of their lunch.

Dodger was ahead, but I soon caught him as an alluring spot on the river had sidetracked him. Flat rocks were basking in the sun with several channels of water flowing in between the sheets of rock. We dropped our packs, and I went swimming in the frigid water. It wasn't too long before I was lounging on the rocks, drying and warming like a reptile in the sun. I lay there gazing at the perfect blue sky, dangling my feet in the cold water and pondering the simple lifestyle of days gone-by.

My mind soon switched gears as I watched the little channels of water running through the rocks. Hundreds of mussels clung to the sides of the rock. The little channel of water is their ecosystem, their world. The channel provides everything the mussels need for their life. I looked out at the surrounding forest. The Cumberland River is part of a major ecosystem—the ecosystem of Daniel Boone National Forest. It plays a major part in the life and well-being of millions of creatures, including the people around it. The river eventually empties its waters into the Ohio River near Paducah, Kentucky, which flows on to the Mississippi another forty miles downstream. What goes on in the Cumberland River has an impact on the Gulf of Mexico, as its waters will eventually find their way there. It all ties together. What a small world.

That night Dodger chose to sleep out in the open on a flat rock near the river while I pitched my tent in the grassy field. That night something infested Dodgers sleeping bag and he suffered hundreds of insect bites.

By morning Dodger was a wreck and was thrilled to see the sun rise. I enjoyed a splendid walk that morning, leaving the Cumberland River and headed up Indian Creek, one of its many tributaries. Along the creek, I jumped several turkeys from their perches atop the trees. The pine trees were a mess however, having suffered major damage from the southern pine beetles. The beetles enter the pines through the soft bark and then eat the base of the bark structure until the bark falls from the tree, eventually killing it. The southern pine beetle is a native species but rarely exist in numbers great enough to do the damage that has been experienced here.

Dodger, as was often the case, was ahead of me. The trail eventually left the stream and continued along the ridge top. I passed several unmarked trail junctions. Repeatedly, I made the best choice I could with the information at hand. I knew I was making the same choices as Dodger until I was suddenly walking into spider webs. That meant the trail had not been traveled in a while. I was pretty sure I knew were I would end up, and at twelve-thirty that afternoon I popped out of the woods at the Barren Fork Horse Campground, three miles south of where I should have been.

Just up the road was the Stearns District Forest Service office, so I headed there. I spoke to a ranger who had seen Dodger. It seems that he too had made a wrong turn and gone north of the desired location. The ranger informed me that Dodger was headed my way, so I dropped my pack in the yard outside the office and walked north on the road to meet him. We walked back to the ranger station together, plotting the course that would lead us back to the elusive trail.

The bugs went away through the day, but nightfall brought a new deluge of biting to Dodger's ankles and legs. His sleeping bag was infested and he shook it out repeatedly, but to no relief. It was too cold to sleep without it, and he suffered terribly until sunrise.

The next morning, I hiked about five miles before catching him at the base of the Yamacraw Bridge. He decided to take a side route along a road in hopes of finding a store and medicine for his bites. We split up and planned to meet at Great Meadows Campground—some twenty miles of trail walking for me, and fourteen miles by the road route Dodger would take. I headed south on the trail alone, enjoying the first few miles as the trail followed the Big South Fork River. Suddenly, the trail turned to swamp. With each step my shoes filled with water. I squished my way along, until I happened across a high water route. It took no time to decide to take the detour.

Soon I found myself on high ground along Laurel Ridge. The day was hot and oppressively dry. The southern pine beetle damage was extreme, and I felt like I was walking through a lumberyard. On each side of me lay tree after tree, killed by the beetles and then cut down by the National Forest Service to keep the trail safe to hike. They had cut a path through the fallen trees. This tragedy continued for three or four miles.

I realized I was low on water and welcomed the drop off the ridge into the normally lush valley below. This area, like much of the eastern United States, continued to suffer from drought that year. I finally found a stream with a trickle of water running. I drank up and filled up, hiked out of the valley and onto the next ridge—back into the heat of the day, back to only a sparse canopy to protect me from the sun. I hiked on and on, and it seemed the ridge walk would continue forever.

Along the way I came across the Blevins-Kidd Cemetery. It was a peaceful little family cemetery in the middle of the forest. Mr. Blevins was born in 1882 and passed away in 1983, living to be 101 years old. I thought about the changes he witnessed in his lifetime, from horse and buggy to flight, to space travel. From telegraph to telephone to computers. From stories told on a Saturday night to radio to motion pictures and television.

At twenty past six I finally reached the end of the ridge. I still had nearly five miles to go and only an hour of daylight. I considered my options. The first 2.6 miles would lead me to a picnic area and the campground road. I could road walk if necessary. Off I went down into the valley to hike along the Mark Branch Creek…or through it. The trail crossed the creek seventeen times in less than two miles. The hollow is not wide enough to support both a trail and a stream, so the two share ground. I passed through the beautiful valley; rock-hopping the stream without getting wet, thanks to the drought. I passed the eighty-foot high Mark Branch falls, which had been reduced to a mere trickle. The area is also home to several impressive natural rock structures.

Rhododendron filled the valley, and I imagined what the view must be like when their flowers are all in bloom. I reached the edge of the picnic area, and the road at ten past seven. I could see the road—it was just over there—over there across a new stream, a deep wide stream. Crossing it was not necessary, unless I wanted to walk the road, which would be easier in the dark. Crossing it would certainly mean getting wet. I still had over two miles to go as dusk began to fall.

I put my feet on auto-pilot and my eyes on night vision, and cruised through this stretch of trail as if it were noon. I was in a serious hiking zone and reached the campground at ten minutes before eight. I never felt the need to get my flashlight out, as the trail was a joy to hike. It was laid out wonderfully, and I could look at the silhouette of the terrain and know where the trail was about to go. The only problem was that the campground was just over there— across the stream. I could see campfires and people from the trail, but nowhere did the trail give me a clue as to where a hiker might gain access to this wonderful National Forest Service campground. Well I did what hikers do best. I found a way: rock-hopping the stream in the darkness. I got a little wet, but it was nothing I couldn't handle.

I entered the campground and looked to my left to see a small flashlight, I gave a little yell: "Dodger."

He was glad to see me and a bit surprised, as it was very dark. He had been able to get some medicine for his bites and felt confident he had cleaned his sleeping bag and gear, ridding himself of the stowaways. He was bug-free. Dodger was told that they were seed ticks which are rampant in the area.

During dinner, I felt an itch on my legs. I shined my flashlight and looked to discover that I had several of the little critters on me. I quickly concurred that they were indeed rampant, as I must have had fifty of them on me between both ankles'. I borrowed Dodger's tweezers and pulled them out, one by one. They are so small you could fit four or five of them on the head of a pin. After I removed them all, I rubbed both ankles with the Campho-Phenique oil that Dodger had acquired earlier in the day.

My body was stiff when I awoke the next morning. The previous twenty five mile day had taken its toll. I had hiked over six hundred miles through Ohio and Kentucky. I had slept next to the Muskingum, Scioto, Ohio, Kentucky and Tennessee rivers. I had met people from all walks of life, had been invited to join in picnics, and had spent the night in their homes. I had made many new friends, witnessed a gunfight, and seen a moonbow. I was certainly seeing the America I sought. I was ready to hike into Tennessee, to see what adventure she might hold for me.

Tennessee & Alabama

Waking to very wet campground compliments of the night's heavy dew only compounded the stiffness in my joints. I was ready to get moving, but wisely decided to let the morning sun work her magic, drying my tent and warming my bones. Dodger and I sat around the picnic table swapping memories of our many miles together. The lightweight backpacking tents we carry dry very quickly and we were on our way by midmorning.

We reached the Tennessee State line before noon, and quietly left Daniel Boone National Forest and Kentucky behind. We slowly hiked the last eight or so miles of the Sheltowee Trace trail, which ran through the Big South Fork National Recreation area. We were in no great hurry knowing that when we finished this section of trail we would be back onto the pavement. It was a garrulous afternoon spent among the tall hardwood trees, sauntering as if we had nary a care in the world. Finally emerging at Pickett State Park we debated if we should stay there or push on a bit farther. We were out of food, and when we found out the park has no amenities of any kind, it made the decision easy.

We walked another four miles or so, before stopping at the Wildwood Lodge Bed & Breakfast, run by Reginald & Julia Johnson, two Brits who moved here eleven years ago to enjoy the vast open spaces of America. We desperately needed laundry done and Julia happily agreed to do it for us, certainly not a normal service provided to their B&B guests. She even gave us each a bathrobe to wear while our wardrobes were being washed. We enjoyed dinner that evening with our hosts and their other guests, treated to a feast of grilled rabbit and pork as well as a bounty of side dishes.

We spent the next several days ambling the back roads of Tennessee towards the town of Sparta, where my Aunt Marie lives. The mornings turned cold and I started each day bundled in most of the clothing I owned; fleece hat and gloves, long pants, long shirt and fleece top. The days warmed quickly, and usually by late morning I was in short pants and t-shirt. The trees were slowly changing from summer green to their glorious fall coats of red, yellow, purple and orange.

As we reached the outskirts of Jamestown, another cold rainstorm was approaching from the west. We made our way to the historic Mark Twain Inn, an older hotel that had seen its better years. I was unsure of the connection with Mark Twain. Nonetheless, that was the name of the old place. There was no front desk, nor a lobby. There was simply a note by the payphone outside. We called the number and waited in the small foyer, trying to keep dry from the falling rain. We shared the foyer with the local drunk, waiting for his cab to take him "uptown"

It was nearly fifteen minutes before our hostess arrived, along with her daughter. She showed us our room, and after hearing about our adventure, treated us to free sodas and candy bars. Dodger and I watched, as Barry Bonds made history, hitting his 71st and 72nd homeruns of the season. It was a good night to be inside as the rains fell long and hard outside.

The next morning the weather turned cold and windy, and we left the hotel bundled up. The day did not warm up today –the thermometer barely broke fifty. The power and warmth of the summer sun was now gone.

Later that afternoon we reached a small grocery store that a young couple was just opening up. We chatted with the proud entrepreneurs while eating chilidogs and chips for dinner. We wished them the best of luck before heading out to find a campsite. We did not have to go far before we found a large open field. We crossed it to the back edge near the woods and pitched our tents at dusk.

We woke to find our tents covered with a thin coating of ice. Our goal for the day was the town of Monterey, twenty-eight miles away. We had no time to let the sun work her magic, so we scraped as much ice off the tent walls as we could. Next came the chore of stuffing the still frozen tents into their carry bags. My fingers went numb in the process. I stood with my hands tucked in against my belly, as I watched Dodger disappear into the early morning fog, just ahead of me.

I again started the day hiking with all of my clothes on, but the fog soon lifted and it turned into a gorgeous fall day with blue skies and temperatures in the sixties. The view from the valley looking up at the surrounding mountains was joyous as the trees continued to put on their multicolored fall coats. I hiked until the valley ended, then climbed the mountains I had spent my morning marveling. I hiked over twelve miles before stopping for a lunch of tortilla and cheese sandwiches. I had not seen Dodger since he slipped into the fog early that morning. As I resumed my hike across the ridge I wondered where he might have gone.

I passed by a house and was greeted by a barking dog, as usual. It seems almost every house has a dog, and they all feel compelled to earn their keep, announcing whenever a stranger passes by. Soon a man dressed in worn blue pants and a white t-shirt stepped to the porch to quiet the dog. He informed me that we had begun attacking Afghanistan.

In the next twenty minutes we talked about our respective times in the military; he had served in Vietnam and I was involved in the conflict with Libya in 1986. He wished me well and I soon found myself trekking along the ridge crest alone again, my mind full of thoughts about the future and the past.

My mind wandered back to the Easter church services onboard the carrier that spring morning in 1986. It was just a few days after we had finished the bombing raid on Libya. I remember listening to the captain speak over the ship's PA system, and the chaplain offering the evening prayers. I remembered, all too well, the sight of live bomb after live bomb being loaded on the fighter and attack jets. I smelled the jet fuel mixed with the salt air and felt the wind blowing hard across the flight deck. I peered out into the endless black Mediterranean night, knowing as our pilots left one by one, they might not return this night. The constant sound of the four steam driven catapults lasted nearly an hour as forty seven jets were launched—all fully loaded I watched the glow of the F-14 afterburners fade out of view into the hostile darkness and then sat waiting for several hours to see our boys come home, which by the grace of God, they all did.

I thought about the thousands of American service men and women who would be going through this same intense ordeal, to avenge and attack on American people. I drifted back to that morning service on the flight deck, only now my prayers were for the men and women fighting to protect me.

My daydream was interrupted about two miles north of Monterey when I finally saw Dodger hiking back out of town towards me. He had just hiked twenty-eight miles and was coming back in search of me, wondering what might have happened to me. I had slowed down somewhat with my mind in overload. Sunset was approaching and he was worried. That is a friend.

When we reached town I called my Aunt Marie who lives nearby. I felt the need to be with family and did not want to wait a few more days. We waited at the edge of town as the sun set and the air again chilled. Soon enough, my aunt and cousin Donna showed up and we were riding in a car, something we had not done in quiet a while. I had not seen them since visiting my dying Uncle Buddy several years earlier.

Having much family news to catch up on, Dodger and I spent the better part of four days there. We helped to get the house ready for winter and day hiked the rest of the way to her house. I finally received my mail from Morehead Kentucky, as I had it forwarded here. It was a well-deserved rest; we had covered 380 miles in the preceding twenty-six days.

During one of the day hikes, I passed by a small country cemetery and noticed a historical marker, so I stopped to learn more. The cemetery was the final resting place for several confederate soldiers, each gravestone emblazoned with C.S.A. proudly identifying each soldier as a fallen member of the Confederate States of America. Each grave also had a faded and tattered Confederate flag, still standing guard. I noticed the headstone of Captain Champ Ferguson.

Ferguson served as a scout for General John Morgan's Cavalry, known as *Morgan's Raiders*, as well as commanded his own regiment. He and Morgan, who were viewed as bandits and scoundrels in the north were heroes here, as they were usually the only line of defense between the Union Army and the citizens of Tennessee. The war, known as the Civil War in the north is "The War of Northern Aggression" in the South.

On Oct. 3, 1864, the Confederate forces in Saltville, Virginia discovered that the Union Army had withdrawn from the field, leaving behind their wounded soldiers. They were left in field hospitals or on the battlefield where they had fallen. Nearly all of the wounded were African-American soldiers, many of whom were recruited straight out of slavery only weeks before. Early that October morning the Confederate soldiers executed an unknown number of wounded Union soldiers. Estimates range from a dozen, to as many as 155. At the time, Confederate soldiers were under orders to execute any blacks they captured in a Union Army uniform, on charges of treason.

Champ Ferguson surrendered under a verbal promise of parole on May 23, 1865; and the federal cavalry captured him three days later at his home. He was then taken to Nashville to stand trial for war crimes. Federal reports charged Ferguson with personally committing fifty-three murders. He was essentially denied the right to any defense and was convicted of killing one white Union officer, Lieutenant Smith of the 13th Kentucky Cavalry. Champ Ferguson was hung on October 20th, 1865. He was one of only two people hung for war crimes in the Civil War; the other being the notorious Andersonville Prison Camp Commander, Henry Wirtz

Before his execution, he requested that he be buried in White County; in the land he had fought so bravely to defend, in the land that he loved. I stayed there for some time and found the place to have an incredible energy. It was an emotional experience to say the least.

Later in the day, I saw my first stand of Kudzu. Kudzu is a non-native vine that was introduced in the United States in 1876. During the Great Depression, the Soil Conservation Service promoted the Japanese native vine for erosion control. Hundreds of men were put to work planting kudzu through the Civilian Conservation Corps. Later in the 1940's farmers were paid as much as eight dollars an acre to plant fields of the vines. Today it covers over seven million acres of land in the southeastern US. The problem is that it grows too well. The vines have been known to grow a foot a day during the summer months. It will climb trees, power poles, houses and to anything else it can attach. Don't get caught standing too long in the southern forest; the vines can grow sixty feet a year. While they help prevent erosion, they also destroy valuable forests by stealing all of the sunlight.

Even though the weather forecast was not good, the time had come to bid my family farewell and get back on the trail. We took a few pictures to capture the visit in the annals of family history, passed the good-bye hugs all around and Dodger and I were off. We had 110 miles to the Natchez Trace Parkway, our next major path.

The skies remained dishwater grey for the next several days, and the rains fell intermittently. When you hike in the forest, the trees stop most of the rain as well as the wind. On the open road, it is much different. You get the full force of the wind and rain, as well as the generated wind and rain from the passing cars. Then again, cars are not so bad—semi-trucks bring the experience to another level. Oftentimes you stop walking and turn your back to avoid the onrush of dirty water thrown at you. Even so, Dodger and I trudged on, enjoying our freedom and meeting our countrymen.

One grey afternoon as Dodger and I passed through the small rural town of Smithville, I checked my email. I carried a device known as Pocketmail, and it allowed me to check my email wirelessly, via telephone. Dodger and I were sitting in the local diner, eating lunch and watching the rain fall outside. I received a message from Mat Olson. Mat runs the website Trailjournals.com, where I kept an online journal. He informed me I was being sought out for a television show. The TV show is called *Radical Sabbatical* and the focus is on people who have given up the security of a good corporate job to chase dreams. I thought to myself, I certainly fit that bill.

I discussed the opportunity with Dodger and then called the Weller Grossman offices in Los Angeles. I did a phone interview with one of the show's producers; she seemed interested and informed me they would get back in touch with me.

Dodger and I left town in the rain, just as we had walked in, only now I was as giddy as a kid at Christmas. I talked Dodger's ear off about the possibilities that being on TV might hold. It seemed like an incredible opportunity. They wanted Dodger to be a part of the show also, since he certainly was a very large part of the adventure.

The next morning the skies were grey, but it was dry. The forecast called for heavy thunderstorms and tornado warnings at night however. We were thirty-two miles away from Murfreesboro--farther than I had ever hiked in one day. As normal, Dodger was out ahead of me. I was trudging along when I noticed some chaffing between my thighs. It seemed to get worse with each step, and was certainly a painful distraction.

I knew I had to do something if I wanted to hike much farther, let alone another twenty-five miles. I found a few bushes and snuck inside to apply some Gold Bond powder. I hiked on another mile but things were only going from bad to worse. With every step, I was rubbing my legs raw. I started to think that the new pair of pants I had gotten in the mail while at my Aunt's house might be the cause of my problem.

I desperately needed to find a place to change my pants. This is no big deal in the morning while in your tent.

Trying to find a spot to change your pants along a busy, populated highway, without being arrested is another challenge. I finally found an old cemetery sitting on a small round hill. I walked to the back, out of view thanks to the crest of the hill, out of view so long as no cars came down the small country lane next to it.

I quickly changed my pants with no issues and was hiking again. I could tell an immediate difference; hopefully I had not chaffed too badly before making the change.

A few miles down the road, I reached another historical marker indicating the sight of yet another battle between General Morgan and the Federalists. I stopped and looked at the surrounding hills, daydreaming of that April day in 1863 when the forest was filled with the sounds of cannons and muskets, and the air was heavy with the smoke of the spent black powder. I wondered what it must have been like to be a civilian in that area, hiding the children in the root cellar and praying that the fighting did not come closer, praying that all of the men would return home. I wondered if that was the same fright the people of Afghanistan were experiencing at that moment.

I caught up with Dodger in the late afternoon, sitting at a small store. We had twenty-five miles in and seven to go. With the days being so short and daylight at a premium, we debated if we should try to find a campsite or push on into town. Dodger thought that watching a tornado from the tents would be a great experience. We decided to push to seek the relative safety of a hotel. About three miles from town the rains started, and quickly upgraded from gentle to heavy. It was a cold rain and the wind soon picked up. I had blistered my left little toe as well as wearing my inner thighs raw. We slogged along through the rain, much slower than our normal three miles per hour. We finally saw the glowing sign of the hotel as the day's last light was fading away. The

long hot shower that night felt incredible. The storm raged
all night and as I lie awake in bed, I knew we had made the
right decision.

The weather now better and the Natchez Trace
Parkway drawing ever closer, I saw my first cotton field. It
was a beautiful sight: millions of tiny white balls of cotton
emanating from the brown background of dirt and dying
plants.

They say that cotton is the fabric of our lives. This
may be true for those living in town, but when you're living
on the land, the rule of thumb is cotton kills. The only cotton
objects I carried were three bandanas. The drawback to
cotton in the backcountry is three fold; when it gets wet it
becomes very heavy, dries slow and loses eighty percent of
it's insulating ability. It is a wonderful fabric, but not
practical for wintertime in the outdoors.

As we passed through the small town of Snell,
Dodger met a guy hitchhiking. The man stopped him and
asked "Hey can you take me to Woodbury."

Dodger looked at him in amazement and muttered a
confused "WHAT?"

"Can you take me to Woodbury? I need a ride to
Woodbury."

"And just what do you suggest I give you a ride in?
Do you want to climb on my back? Can't you see that I am
walking?" The man looked dumbfounded, in absolute
disbelief that we didn't have a car. We chuckled to
ourselves as we walked on, reaching the town of Franklin
late that afternoon.

Early the next morning we headed out of Franklin,
our last town before starting our trek of the Natchez Trace.
While still in town, I stopped at a historical site to learn
about the Choctaw Treaty that had been held in the spring of
1830. President Andrew Jackson attended the treaty, the

only removal treaty ever attended by a president. It led to
the removal of the Choctaw nation to Indian country in
Oklahoma. The removal of the Creek, Chickasaw, and
Cherokee soon followed.

President Andrew Jackson's Indian Policy remains a
dark cloud in our history. The Indian Nations affected by it
have never rebounded to their original level of prosperity.
These nations had been peaceful to the Americans and
embraced many of the white ways, including developing an
alphabet, farming and Christianity. They were removed
anyhow under President Jackson's orders.

About four miles from the entrance to the Natchez
Trace Parkway, I caught up with Dodger sitting at the end of
a long driveway. I looked up the windy gravel road and
could see why he was waiting for me. The mansion at the
top was breathtaking, beckoning him to stop and see it. The
large old structure looked like a capitol building, having a
large dome. Dodger had set his heart on seeing the inside of
it; I just wanted to get onto the Natchez Trace. I soon found
myself walking up the drive with Dodger, hoping to find
someone home. The large wooden front door commanded
respect, standing eight feet high or better. The age-old
bricks that made up the house had hundreds of stories to tell,
but they kept their silence, giving none of the secrets of this
magnificent old palace. We knocked on the door, but no one
came. We sat on the front porch enjoying lunch, hoping
someone would soon return.

An hour passed and still no one was home. Dodger
refused to leave, he felt committed to seeing the inside. I
became restless and pushed on to the parkway, agreeing to
wait for him at the entrance. I covered the four miles in just
over an hour, and then sat to wait for Dodger. I found a
visitors information stand there and picked up a brochure to
learn more about the trail that lie ahead. The brochure read:

*The Natchez Trace is a story of people
on the move, of the age-old need to get from
one place to another. It is a story of Natchez,
Chickasaw, and Choctaw Indians following
traditional ways of life, of French and
Spanish people venturing into a world new to
them, and of people building a new nation. At
first the trace was probably a series of
hunters' paths that slowly came to form a trail
from the Mississippi over the low hills into the
valley of the Tennessee. By 1733, the French
knew the land well enough to map it and
showed an Indian trail running from Natchez
to the Northeast. By 1785, Ohio River Valley
farmers searching for markets had begun
floating their crops and products down the
rivers to Natchez or New Orleans. Because
they sold their flatboats for lumber, returning
home meant either riding or walking. The
trail from Natchez was the most direct.*

*Growing numbers of travelers
tramped the crude trail into a clearly marked
path. By 1810, many years of improvements
had made the trace an important wilderness
road, the most heavily traveled in the Old
Southwest. Many Inns, locally called stands,
were built. By 1820, more than 20 stands
were in operation. Most provided no more
than shelter and plain food, although the
stands at Mount Locust and Red Bluff were
substantial, well known establishments. Even
with these, the trace was not free of
discomforts. Thieves added an element of*

*danger to a catalog of hazards that included
swamps, floods, disease-carrying insects and
sometimes-unfriendly Indians. A new chapter
in transportation dawned in January 1812
when the Steamer New Orleans arrived in
Natchez. Within a few years, steamboat was
the preferred method of travel. Soon the
bustle of the Trace had quieted to the
peacefulness of a forest lane.*

I was ready to being hiking the Trace. I looked
forward to it since I started planning the adventure. There I
sat at the entrance and I could not enter. Keeping my word
to Dodger, I sat for over two hours patiently waiting as the
day slowly passed.

Dodger finally arrived at five. He was very excited,
and I was upset. He had gotten in to see the house, meeting
the woman who owned it. She had sat and had a glass of
wine with him, telling of the history of the old place. Onto
the parkway we hiked, Dodger with a jump in his step, me
grumbling about not getting as far as I had wanted. We
came onto the parkway four miles south of the northern
terminus, and I wanted to hike every inch of it. So north we
went. After hiking just over a mile Dodger found a campsite
and stopped. I was still determined to reach the northern
terminus today and informed him I was going to hike on. I
reached the north end at dusk, three miles from where I had
left Dodger. I took a picture for proof and then decided to
night hike the three miles back. The sunset was spectacular
and the sky glowed with reds and purples. Soon the sky was
illuminated by millions of stars and I strolled along the road,
enjoying the peacefulness that pervades the parkway. The
walk alone calmed me and I realized I had been pretty rough

on Dodger, allowing my anger to overflow at his side adventure. Had I forgotten the reason we were even here?

I reached the campsite at about 7:20 but couldn't find Dodger. I walked deeper into the woods, calling his name repeatedly, but there was no answer. I had no clue where to look next so I decided to camp alone, the first night on the adventure we camped apart. I set up my tent and cooked dinner. I sat alone in the chilly night air watching the stars as I finished my pot of Lipton noodles. After a quick washing of the pot, I crawled into my tent hoping I would find Dodger in the morning.

I was up at sunrise to another cold frosty morning. As I hoisted my pack under deep blue skies, I saw two deer crossing the parkway below me. The morning sun was quickly warming the air and it was a perfect day for hiking. I headed out alone, not sure if I would find Dodger or if I had angered him with my impatience.

I hiked the entire morning alone with no sign of Dodger anywhere. Around noon I reached a Ranger Station where I stopped to check in. I wanted to let them know I would be hiking their parkway for the next several weeks. They had not seen Dodger. Had he left the Trace where we had come on? Was he on his way back to Oklahoma?

I pressed on southward mumbling to myself when a small pickup pulled beside me. The couple inside had just left Dodger at the picnic area another mile down the road. He had sent them looking for me. They offered me a ride south to meet him, but I refused the ride explaining the purpose of the walk. I arrived at the Garrison Creek Picnic area about 20 minutes later to find Dodger and our new friends. It was now almost 1 PM, and I was hungry. I made two cheese and tortilla sandwiches, and our friends offered me a banana and a pop. Our friends soon drove off and Dodger and I sat down and discussed the last 24 hours. We worked out our disagreement and soon were laughing, ready to again hike.

Just south of the rest area, we passed the Tennessee Valley Divide. When Tennessee joined the Union in 1796, it was the boundary between the state of Tennessee and the Chickasaw Nation to the south. We spent the next several days hiking in Chickasaw country.

As we hiked, a man passed us going north on a bike. He returned a little later and stopped to ask if we needed a place to stay the night. He owned property not far away, just off the parkway and we could camp there. We decided to take him up on the offer, arriving at dusk to find a log cabin at the edge of the recently plowed fields, just as he had described it. The cabin was nice, but was used as a storage shed and was not suitable for us to sleep in, so we pitched our tents in the yard.

The next day found us sitting at Jackson Falls, named for President Andrew Jackson. The two-tiered falls are a splendid sight as they roll down the rock-faced ledge, sparkling and bouncing off the rugged creek bottom. We sat enjoying the peacefulness of the area for some time. Soon the tranquility ended as three ladies and their children arrived. The kids, all seven of them, were full of energy and curiosity as they explored the place. It was good to see kids in the outdoors enjoying themselves so much.

Later that day I came to a two-mile section of the original Trace. As I walked along I drifted back in time. I was a farmer returning from Natchez where I had recently sold my crops. I had my full year's salary on me and was trying to make it home. I felt pretty safe as I was close to Nashville now, but still in Chickasaw country, several miles south of the Tennessee State line. The Chickasaw had agreed by treaty to allow travelers safe passage through here and, generally speaking, they would not attack. I walked alone through the forest, I heard a loud crack—then a boom as a tree fell in the forest near me. I was startled as the forest again fell silent, the tree down. The crash brought me back to the present and I walked on smiling inside at my little journey back in time.

Soon I reappeared on the parkway and found Dodger resting at an old tobacco barn. Now a museum, it was set up with tobacco drying and signs explaining the arduous labor involved in tobacco farming. To farm tobacco it takes about 250 man-hours per acre from planting to harvesting. Compared to just three hours an acre for wheat, that is a lot of time.

We stopped for the night on another section of the old Trace. After enjoying dinner, Dodger and I watched the sunset. It was nothing spectacular, but the show afterwards in the night sky was. The moon hung low in the western sky, a sliver of brilliant yellow illuminating its outline. Soon Mars appeared brilliant in the southern sky and then I saw my old friend Orion the Hunter high in the southern sky--a sure sign that winter is not far off. The stars soon covered the clear crisp night sky and the owls arrived to "who, who" me to sleep.

I woke up at about 7:30 under a brilliant red sunrise. The morning was made for hiking; the sky a deep blue and the forest around me silent except for the wind whooshing through the trees. A few miles into the day's adventure I found myself standing at the old Sheboss Inn grounds. There were Inns all along the old Trace, built about a day's travel apart. In Chickasaw country they were owned and operated by Chickasaws. An Indian who was married to a white woman owned The Sheboss Inn. He spoke little English, and when a traveler stopped, he would point to his wife and say "She boss." She then took care of the business. That is how the place got its name. Nothing is left of the old stand, just a well kept grassy area where it once stood and the silence of stories longing to be told.

That afternoon we arrived at the Meriwether Lewis Campground, the site where Meriwether Lewis is buried. He died at the age of thirty-five on Oct 11, 1809, under very mysterious circumstances at Robert Grinder's Stand, another of the inns along the Trace. Lewis traveled there on his way to Washington, DC. He was distraught over his duties as the first Governor of the new Louisiana Territory. It is said that he was not mentally stable. On the night of October 10, two gunshots were heard. The innkeeper was too fearful to leave her quarters. The next morning, Lewis was found clinging to life; he had two wounds: one to his head and one to his chest. He died later that day.

By the age of thirty-five, Meriwether Lewis had accomplished more in his life than most could ever imagine He was a woodsman, soldier, adventurer, personal secretary to President Jefferson, co-captain of the Lewis and Clark expedition, and the first Governor of the Louisiana Territory. Did a man who accomplished so much take his own life, or was foul play involved? This is certainly one of America's greatest unsolved mysteries.

Jefferson spoke this of him: "His courage was undaunted; His firmness and Perseverance Yielded to Nothing but Impossibilities; a Rigid Disciplinarian, yet Tender as a Father of Those Committed to his Charge; Honest, Disinterested, Liberal, with a sound Understanding and a Scrupulous Fidelity to Truth."

The next morning I again passed the grave of Meriwether Lewis and stood in awe at the accomplishments of this remarkable man. I trekked on, finally taking a break late in the morning. As I sat at a picnic area, a lone bike rider named Henry appeared and I was soon side tracked into a wonderful conversation. We said goodbye and Henry informed that I would probably catch his group since they were taking their time. I laughed and said I didn't think I would be keeping up with a group of cross-country bikers.

Two miles later, I found Henry and his two friends, Ron and Anne. They had stopped to rest and the repartee that ensued lifted my spirits higher than they already were. We chatted for over an hour with the main topic being the simple joy of being a hobo and traveling about. They too were on a great journey, biking the entire Natchez Trace and then some. They had come from all over the world to explore together; Anne from England, Ron from Alabama, and Henry from Delaware.

All good things must end, and soon enough I was hiking on. Anne passed me, then Ron, and finally Henry. I was again alone and I hiked in the peace and quiet that surrounds the age old trace. I be-bopped along at my three miles an hour just overjoyed at being there and being able to live this adventure.

Soon a few southbound motorcycles passed me and pulled over just in front of me. I caught up to them and asked if they were okay. One rider had received a bee sting and they asked if I had anything for first aid. Fortunately, I had some cortisone cream and was able to help. My good deed done for the day, I was pounding the pavement wondering how far I was behind Dodger . I laughed and hiked, just bubbly with happiness. It was a day that could not get any better.

I floated along for several more miles, finally catching Dodger at a road crossing. He had found a store and had a Mountain Dew for me. As we walked back to the store we noticed a motel sign on the horizon. It had been more than a hundred miles since the last bath, so we pushed on and were soon sitting at the Natchez Trace Motel. It was a nice old place, but will soon be gone as they are widening the road and it is in the way. Such is the price of progress.

We reached the Alabama state line the next morning--our fourth state. We had been told there was a store at the state line but we saw no road and no store. We had planned on getting breakfast there so we stopped a truck at the next crossroad.

"Well now there is a new place over on route eight, but that's a far piece from here," the guy in the truck noted.

"Well just how far a piece might that be?" I questioned.

"I reckon you go south about four miles then take a right onto Route eight for a mile or so."

We pushed on, growing hungrier by the step. As we reached route eight a car pulled to the stop sign. We asked about the directions, and were assured it was just ahead. A mile later and just like magic a store appeared--Threets Treats. It was their grand opening. Inside, we met Madeline, the young lady who had given us directions, her mother Alicia, and her Great Aunt. Madeline's Great Aunt started the store many years before but had to shut it down about three years ago. Alicia was opening it up again. We were two of the first customers and the only two in the store at the time.

When you hike, your appetite can get out of hand, like a hungry caterpillar. We decided to try out the menu. I had a cheeseburger and fries, as well as some incredible beans and corn bread, all washed down with sweet tea. In the South, sweet tea rules. You have to request unsweetened tea. After we finished, Madeline asked if we had room for desert--homemade pecan pie and ice cream. How can you say no to that offer? Simply put, it was the best pecan pie I had ever had; so good in fact, that Dodger had seconds.

We bought some food for the trail, chatted with the proud owners for a bit, and took some photos. By this time business had picked up and we left them with a full house. We then hiked the mile back to the Trace. We both agreed that the pie alone was worth the two extra miles.

We hiked the rest of the day before reaching the mighty Tennessee River. We set out across the mile-long bridge. We stopped at the pinnacle where we noticed a joist where the two sides of the bridge meet. There was a gap, perhaps two or three inches wide. In the gap on both sides of the bridge was a colony of bats, all settled in for a long day of rest, waiting for the fall of night and feeding time. It is amazing how wildlife adapts to its environment. There were also plenty of spiders on the bridge, their webs dancing in the constant breeze that blows through the valley. They were hunting the same thing as the bats--bugs.

We reached the other side and the Colbert Ferry Campground where we met Derrick Southard the ranger. He was helpful and chatted with us for a while, telling us of the local history of the place.

We set up camp and enjoyed dinner before going to find the location of Colbert's Stand, another inn on the old Trace. Located along the river, George Colbert owned the stand and ran a ferry service to get people across the river. The river was only about a quarter mile wide then, and the most dangerous crossing on the entire Trace.

His brother William Colbert was a private in Jackson's army and was slightly wounded at the battle of the "Horse Shoe" in the Creek Nation, he was then a very old man but was brave and fond of the army, would often boast of his bravery and his friendship for the white man.

Legend has it George charged General Jackson $75,000 to ferry his army across the river. The location of the inn can still be seen. It was captivating to sit at the site as the sun fell and think of what the place must have been like on a fall afternoon in 1810. I pictured Indians and settlers trading and talking, milling about the busy little stand. The hot summer sun setting then much as it was tonight, the mosquitoes buzzing about and men fishing in the river. The place had a special energy to it.

I received an email from Kasie, the high school student who was our waitress at the Ponderosa Steakhouse in Morehead, Kentucky. In her note, she wrote that she had long held a dream of being a model, but had been told by friends and family she couldn't do that. She thanked me for giving her the inspiration, and courage to chase her dream. Her first modeling show would be held in early November. As I read the letter, I cried.

When I left Ohio, I had come for me. I had not considered what an impact my journey might have on other people; that by chasing my dream I might encourage other people to do the same. I didn't realize as I strengthened my belief in humanity, that I would also be strengthening the faith of those I met as well. The walk was beginning to have a greater purpose.

The Mississippi State line was twenty miles away, and that was our destination for the day. Seven miles into the trek we reached Buzzard Roost Spring where George Colbert's brother, Levi operated a stand. Levi was the principle chief of the Chickasaw and sat in council several treaties with the United States, including the removal treaty of 1830. The treaty he agreed to was that the Chickasaw would go west when suitable lands were provided for them. The prairie home they were given was not what they had in mind and on February 23, 1832, Levi Colbert addressed the president, saying the Chickasaw were not ready to migrate and that the treaty was not valid.

He said the land "...which the Choctaw perhaps will let us have, is most of it big prairies, mighty little wood, water, or good land; it will be mighty hard for my people to live there... it was the words in your message which alarmed and roused the fears of my people; you speak of this treaty as final, this is not the sense of it; we have not got as yet any home in the west... you can see the strong and marked difference of our condition here and in the wild distant regions of the west, surrounded by none but distance and deer trade and warlike tribes thrown together."

In the 1800's historian L.C Draper worked hard to capture factual evidence of the American west. He had written to a Mr. J.N. Walton who had known Levi Colbert well. He replied to Mr. Draper concerning the old chief:

> *Although he had a plurality of wives,*
> *nevertheless he had an intellect far superior*
> *to the common mass of people without regard*
> *to color or nationality, he was shrew and*
> *influential among his tribe, in fact his words*
> *or advice was the law among them, his people*
> *loved him, the Chiefs, Captains, with their*
> *King, looked up to him: his speeches in the*
> *councils would electrify them and throw them*
> *almost into ecstasies. I have heard him speak*
> *in council often, and although I could but*
> *partially understand their language, I could*
> *understand enough to know that his*
> *eloquence might well be compared to Henry*
> *Clay and Mr. Webster or any one else, his*
> *eyes would glow with brightness, his gestures*
> *were so sublime that they seemed to*

*[unreadable] what he was about to say, his
Indian name was It-a-wam-ba Mingo
(meaning) Setting King. He was kind and
generous to a fault, liberal in all dealings,
never out of humor, he loved his friends and
was loved and honored by all who knew him,
he was kind and affectionate to his family,
although he had a number of wives (only
three) and two of them sisters, they lived as
cordial and affectionately as so many sisters.
They would laugh and joke each other as
though they wives of different men, and no
discord ever happened among them.*

He also wrote to Mr. Draper about Tecumseh visiting
the chief and speaking to the Indians in an effort to create an
Indian Nation to fight the Americans,

*The old chief secreted Tecumseh in his cellar &
covered his den with logs & put canes through
the cracks for breathing - till he sent out runners
& got the chiefs in: Then at night they carried
Tecumseh a few hundred yards west to a noted
large oak, where it was said he made a most
eloquent speech, but effected nothing. After the
council, Levi Colbert conveyed him to the
Choctaws; & then he went to the Creeks &
roused part of that nation.*

The spring at Buzzard's Roost still runs and looked
inviting with it's deep clear pool of water. We decided to get
a big drink and fill our water bottles. Dodger walked down
the leaf-covered path towards the spring and when he got
close he found slick mud. His feet quickly slipped out from
beneath him and wham—he fell hard. He got up slowly,
groaning from the sudden impact. He didn't seem to be hurt,

but he sure was muddy. We filled our water bottles and I climbed back to the Trace, hiking south slowly so that Dodger would be sure to catch me. Dodger sat at the spring trying to wash the mud from his body and clothes.

Mississippi

I arrived at the Bear Creek Picnic area to wait for Dodger so we could cross the state line together. He arrived and we chatted before setting out to walk the last four miles to the state line. He was hiking without a limp; the fall didn't seem to have hurt him. We reached the state line around six and took pictures of the occasion. We then hiked another half-mile to the Cave Spring area. The spring still runs, but the water is no longer safe to drink. The area is littered and part of the cave is collapsed, but for thousands of years it was a viable water source.

We set up camp nearby and sat out enjoying dinner while gazing at the endless night sky. I got up and walked towards a fence, all the while gazing up. I stood there not knowing I would soon learn about fire ants. It seems my left foot had disturbed a mound and I quickly felt the burning sensation of bites on my left ankle. A monumental struggle ensued as I quickly moved away and took off my shoe and sock. As I brushed them off my foot, they would cling to my hand and bite. Dodger was laughing at my escapade, watching me hop around on one foot while fighting with the ants. I escaped with about a dozen bites and a lesson well learned. I was no longer in Ohio. I was in the land of black widows and brown recluse spiders; water moccasins, copperhead and rattlesnakes; and of course, fire ants.

Dodger and I now stood on the banks of the Tennessee / Tombigbee waterway. From the early 1800's until about 1910, paddle driven steamboats navigated the free flowing Tombigbee River carrying passengers and goods as far north as Amory, Mississippi, delivering stacks of cotton bales, logs and other commodities. They could only navigate the river when the water was deep enough.

The 450-mile long man made waterway was first discussed in the 1770's and first proposed to congress in 1810. President Grant authorized an engineering investigation during his term, but congress denied the grant to build it, deeming it impractical. As the name suggests, it connects the Tennessee River with the Tombigbee River, cutting the distance from northern Alabama to the Gulf of Mexico by some eight hundred miles. Congress finally approved money to build the waterway in 1946 and it was finally completed in 1984 at a cost of two billion dollars. The fact that it was completed in 1984 is a testament to how important our navigable waterways continue to be in the national economic picture.

Late that afternoon Dodger and I arrived at the ninety-acre site of Pharr Mounds, built by Native Americans of the Hopewell Culture. There are eight different mounds; each a different size ranging from two feet high to eighteen feet high. The mounds seem out of place; mounds of this type are more commonly found in Ohio and Illinois. They were hand built, one basket of earth at a time, over several years. The burial ground is one of the largest ceremonial sites in the Southeast. The National Park Service excavated four of the mounds in 1966. They discovered fire pits and low, clay platforms as well as cremated and unburned human remains. Along with the remains, they found assorted ceremonial artifacts such as copper objects, decorated ceramic vessels, a sheet of mica, and a greenstone platform pipe. These items did not start off in Mississippi, but were brought here through extensive trade networks. They were built around the time Jesus Christ lived. They are magnificent and spiritual—in short, they are awe-inspiring.

We had dinner with the mounds in the background then decided to camp nearby. We pitched our tents then walked out under the dazzling half moon and clear skies to be among the mounds. In the southwestern skies, a storm was approaching. I had heard tornado warnings for the area on my radio, but tonight we had no place to get out of the weather. We would have to trust our gear on this one. We watched as bolt after bolt of lightening lit up the sky, bolt after bolt crashing to earth with a fury that told us we would soon be in a brutal storm. The moon and stars disappeared as the clouds moved in and a short while later the thunder accompanied the lightening. We sat mesmerized in the field, in the midst of the Indian Mounds.

The wind picked up and the rains came down, lightly at first. We ran for our tents, which were a hundred yards away. We arrived just as the rains fell hard. As I crawled into my tent, the tempest was full blown. The storm raged around my single wall tent and me. At times the wind sucked the walls of the tent in so tight that I barely had room to fit. The wind howled and the rain fell, but I stayed dry. After forty-five minutes of intense fury the storm passed. Dodger and I both emerged from our cocoons to watch the lightning show again, now off to the northeast. Soon the clouds too were gone, the moon and stars reappeared, and the tranquility of the night world was restored.

The next morning I was blessed to wake at sunrise. I peered out of my tent at the wet world around me as the sun first appeared on the horizon. Each droplet of water provided a prism for the morning sun to shine through and beyond that magical sight was the eastern sky, set afire with the promise of a new day.

That afternoon brought the discovery of the graves of thirteen unknown Confederate Soldiers buried next to a section of the original Trace. Each white stone stood above the brown decaying leaves that carpeted the forest floor. They were set in a semicircle, each decorated with old plastic flowers and Confederate flags. The place was humbling, beautiful and haunting at the same time.

We stopped in Tupelo for a night to get me a pair of much-needed new shoes. It was a strange feeling being inside a shopping mall, with all of the people and hustle and bustle—a side of life I had not seen in some time.

Just south of Tupelo, Dodger and I reached an extended section of finished Natchez Trace National Scenic Trail. Someday there will be a trail that runs the entire 440 miles, but for now it is complete only in several small sections.

We found ourselves off the highway and hiking through the wooded rolling hills for a few miles. When we emerged from the forest, we came out at the site of one of the many villages of the Chickasaw, where there once stood several houses and a town fort. Their locations were outlined to show the town layout. Dodger disappeared, exploring the area while I sat alone for most of an hour in the center of one of the winter hut locations. I gazed into the endless clear blue sky, the steady hum of the nearby parkway in the background. The wooded hills we had just walked lay to my north and east, while tall prairie grasses blowing in the breeze dominated the south and western lands. I again slipped into my own world, far away from today and dreamed of life here 250 years ago. I dreamed of the daily bustle of Indian life, the gathering of water and wood, the making of clothing and baskets and pottery, the playing of games.

Dodger reappeared and brought me back to today, back to reality, back to the fact that we needed to make more miles. We packed up and headed south until we reached the site of the Tribal Council house, eight miles away, where all significant tribal business was conducted. There were many villages around the area and each would send a representative to the council house when business needed to be discussed. It's where Levi Colbert would have met Tecumseh.

Tecumseh's dream would not come to pass, despite his untiring efforts and the buildup of a large alliance. The plan was done in by the greed of his brother, The Prophet, and the sharp military mind of William Henry Harrison.

The village of Tockshish once stood just south of the old council house. Also known as McIntoshville, it was a community of white men and Indians and was built up around the home of the British Indian agent, John McIntosh, who settled there around 1770. When the old Indian trail was established as a national road in 1801, Tockshish became a relay station where post riders carrying mail between Nashville and Natchez could exchange weary horses for fresh ones. The post riders would then move on with their mailbags. For them it was a five-day journey from there to Nashville and a full seven days to Natchez.

Continuing south along the old Trace, I reached the Monroe Mission, the first Mission to be established in Chickasaw land. Rev. Thomas C. Stuart founded the mission upon his arrival from South Carolina in 1821. His wife had come west with him as well as two men -a mechanic named Vernon and a farmer named Pickens, along with their families. Lessons at the mission included Christianity, general education instruction in farming, carpentry and other skills needed to be successful in "civilized" life.

The Spanish explorer Hernando DeSoto also resided in the area, having spent the winter nearby in 1540-1541, over 460 years ago. He camped near the Chickasaw and then moved on in the spring. In the summer of 1541 he became the first white man to see the mighty Mississippi River, less than fifty years after Columbus discovered the continent.

I felt much like Desoto, discovering America's history as well as her present as I walked along. The days were filled with excitement as each turn led to another learning opportunity. The hike was going just as planned for me, but for Dodger the hike was filled with pain. The fall he had taken back at the Buzzard's Roost Spring had hurt his back more than he wanted to admit, but he was hiking slower and at times limping along. He didn't complain, but I could see a difference. I hoped he would get better soon.

It was late October, almost Halloween, and after a long twenty-seven mile day we arrived at the Witch Dance Campground. There is a large area of ground there that nothing grows on—not even grass. Nothing has ever grown there and legend says that is where the witches once gathered for ceremonies and dances. Their spirits killed the soil, and to this day it is barren. It was a fitting place to be on Halloween weekend.

Dodger said he might not make it that far, but for me to go ahead. I figured he wanted some alone time and agreed to wait for him in the morning. I reached camp at dusk, set up my tent, then started dinner. I peered into the darkness and saw a campfire. I walked across the campground to say "hi" while my dinner finished cooking. I met three local men who had spent the day riding horses on the trails. They invited me to share in the warmth of their fire. I agreed to return after eating dinner. I went back to camp to eat and hope for Dodger's arrival.

When I returned to the fire, four local high school students had joined them. They were out visiting all of the scary spots around the area. We enjoyed a deep conversation about life and chasing dreams, and of course the legend of the Witch Dance. It was well after eight when Dodger came strolling in. He was in good spirits and said he had enjoyed his night hike in. My concern grew, but he said he was ok. We spent the evening at the campfire with enjoying the company of other campers for a change.

On my last day in Chickasaw country, Dodger and I camped at Line Creek, the boundary between the Chickasaw and Choctaw nations. We pitched our tents behind some trees and sat in the dark at the picnic table near the road. The only lights in the forest were slivers of moonlight shining through the trees. We sat chatting, discussing our day and enjoying dinner when a van pulled up. We sat silently, not knowing who it could be. Soon a woman stepped out and walked straight towards us, undoing her pants as she walked. She obviously had no idea we were there and I figured it would be best if I made our presence known. I called out in a very cheery voice, "Well, hello there!"

She stopped dead in her tracks, then quickly turned, running towards the safety of her van, screaming the whole way "There is someone out there! AHHHHHH!"

I could hear her husband laughing as she ran terrified back to the van. She climbed in and yelled, "GO! GO! GO!"

The van quickly drove off. I had the best intentions and certainly did not mean to scare her. Dodger and I laughed about it for days.

The next day led us to the site of the Pigeon Roost trading post. Nathaniel Folsom, along with his Choctaw wife, originally operated it. Their son David Folsom worked hard to promote Indian education as well as Christianity. He later ran the post as his political influence grew. In 1826, he was elected as Chief of the Northeast District of the Choctaw Nation.

The place was named Pigeon Roost, as this was a major stop along the migratory route of the Passenger Pigeons. As they migrated in the spring and fall, they would blacken the skies. In 1813 John James Audubon recorded seeing enormous flocks of passenger pigeons flying south near Louisville Kentucky. In his book The Birds of America, he wrote:

> *Before sunset I reached Louisville,*
> *distant from Hardensburgh fifty-five miles,*
> *the pigeons were still passing in undiminished*
> *number, and continued to do so for three days*
> *in succession. The people were all in arms.*
> *The banks of the Ohio were crowded with*
> *men and boys, incessantly shooting at the*
> *pilgrims, which there flew lower as they*
> *passed the river. Multitudes were thus*
> *destroyed. For a week or more, the*
> *population fed on no other flesh than that of*
> *pigeons, and talked of nothing but pigeons.*

Other tales reveal the mess involved, saying their droppings would fall like snow across the countryside. They would break the branches of the mightiest of trees, crushing them with their massive numbers. They were once the most abundant bird on earth, numbering in the billions. Unfortunately they were also destructive, capable of devastating any size crop field. They were also a favorite meal. Plants sprung up, processing as many as 18,000 birds a day. It was thought they were invincible, but with deforestation and massive hunting their numbers declined.

In 1869 Michigan enacted laws to protect them and in 1878 Pennsylvania followed. It was too late. The last known bird died at the Cincinnati Zoo on September 1, 1914, the last chapter of a great American tragedy.

The good news is that even though we cannot bring the passenger pigeon back, we have learned from our sins. In the past century, we have made prodigious progress as a nation in the fields of conservation, preservation and protection of endangered species.

In town, I learned that there would be a documentary made for a television show concerning the hike. I spoke to the producer for the first time and we decided we would film when I finished the Natchez Trace, from the town of Natchez. I called my friend Nina Baxley who I planned to visit while there to inform her I would have to change my plans. She mentioned she might be able to make the drive north from Plaquemine, Louisiana to see me instead. With my work in town complete, Dodger and I managed a few more miles, reaching the sight of the old Bethel Mission in late afternoon and camped just beyond there in the woods.

Having gone seventy-five miles in my new shoes, I hoped that my foot pain would have gone away, but it got worse. I bought the same size shoe I had started the hike in, but my feet had apparently grown. My little toes were cramped and worn raw, blistering and bleeding daily. Dodger's feet were no better off, having gone over a thousand miles in the same pair. I hobbled into the Hurricane Creek rest area to find Dodger waiting and in pain. His back was bothering him, but not near as badly as his feet. Only four miles south was the town of Kosciusko. We decided to make it a short day and rest there.

We checked into the first hotel and the asked about the location of the stores, which were nowhere to be seen.

"Ahh well they are uptown," the owner informed us.

Dodger hopingly asked, "How far is uptown"
" Bout three miles" was the answer.
We had given most of what our poor feet would take
getting there; another three miles today would be torture.
The owner of the hotel offered to ride us up town, and we
quickly accepted. In town we found a small local shoe store
that carried New Balance, and had the sizes we needed. We
headed back to the hotel to relax.

Kosciusko is the birthplace of Oprah Winfrey and
was named in honor of General Thaddeus Kosciuszky. He
was born in Lithuania, Poland, on February 12, 1746. At the
outbreak of the American Revolution he was serving as a
captain in the Polish army. On borrowed money he came to
the new world to fight for freedom. In 1776, General George
Washington appointed him as a colonel of engineers in the
Continental Army. He was in charge of building the
fortifications at Saratoga, which played a critical role in
winning that battle in 1777. He also designed and built the
fortifications at West Point. In the latter part of the
Revolutionary War, he served under Nathaniel Greene, as an
engineer and a cavalry officer. By the end of the war he had
risen in rank to brigadier general. He returned to Poland to
fight the invading Russians in 1792. In 1794 he had his own
army of nearly five thousand and defeated the Russian army
at Raclawice. He then became the leader of a provisional
Polish government. Six months later, the new government
was overthrown and he found himself imprisoned. He was
pardoned a few years later and returned to the United States
where President Washington, as he had done for so many
revolutionary war veterans, allotted him a five hundred acre
tract of land in Ohio. After several years of imprisonment in
Russia, Kosciuszky was pardoned. He passed away on
October 15, 1817 in Switzerland, and was buried with honors
in Poland.

As evening fell, hunger set in and Dodger thought it a good idea to get some dinner. We both put on the better of our two sets of clothes as well as our new shoes. As I put my second shoe on, it did not fit; it was a left shoe, just like the first one. I guess I could hobble to dinner in the old shoes one more time.

Late the next morning, I caught up with Dodger at the crossroads of the Natchez Trace and Robinson Road. Built in 1821, Robinson road was the second road to be built leading to the old southwest. The development of Robinson road, along with the invention of steam travel, led to the decline in importance of the Natchez Trace.

Early the next day we reached a Cypress Swamp. We spent nearly an hour exploring the dark murky wetland. The dead brown fall leaves sat silently atop the black water as giant tupelo and bald cypress trees emerged, towering high above the rich ecosystem. The pointy knees of the trees' root systems jutted out of the water, rising a foot or so into view. They give stability to the trees, allowing them to grow in the muddy basin. I had never been in a swamp before and felt great contentment there. Everyone should spend an hour in a swamp

I hiked on ahead of Dodger daydreaming and trying to catch leaves as they fell to the ground. I had gone about seven miles when a forest service ranger pulled beside me to chat. He told me Dodger was a few miles back and asked if I needed anything. I asked him about water sources between here and Rocky Springs, some twenty-five miles away. He informed me there was no water. He was on his way to Rocky Springs and offered to take a bottle and drop it off to me on his way back.

I hiked on another mile and stopped at the Battle of Raymond historic site to wait for Dodger. The Battle of Raymond was part of the Vicksburg Campaign during the

Civil War. General Ulysses S. Grant led the Union Army to
a major victory here. After the battle General Grant took his
army about five miles down the Trace to Dean's Stand,
which became his headquarters.

Forty-five minutes later Dodger arrived, hobbled by
his painful back. It seemed to be getting worse-not better.
We were nearly eighty miles from Natchez where we would
have four days off to rest and film for the television show. I
hoped the time off would help him heal. I hoped he would
make it that far.

We hiked together to the site of Dean's Stand. About
a mile before reaching the stand, my ranger friend returned
with enough water to get us to Rocky Springs. He was in a
hurry, and barely stopped long enough to wish us well and
leave the water.

Tall pines still adorn the now quiet desolate area
where William Dean and his wife Margaret built their stand
in 1823; just three years after the United States took this land
via treaty with the Choctaw. After the 1820 treaty many
settlers came rushing into the then southwestern United
States to claim land and settle. The Deans farmed the land
and allowed travelers, mail riders, boatmen, preachers and
others who came along, to lodge in their house.

Part of the old Trace is still visible, having avoided
the development and pavement of the parkway project. Just
east of the road is an old graveyard with graves dating to the
1850s. I bet the place bustled with activity in the 1820s The
Indian policy of the time is well reflected in Article four of
the 1820 treaty with the Choctaw that reads:

The boundaries hereby established
between the Choctaw Indians and the United
States, on this side of the Mississippi river,
shall remain without alteration until the

period at which said nation shall become so
civilized and enlightened as to be made
citizens of the United States, and Congress
shall lay off a limited parcel of land for the
benefit of each family or individual in the
nation.

Another nine miles south, we reached the boundary
line that was established in 1816. The Indians did not lose
their land in a great war; they lost it one piece at a time, in
treaty after treaty that was aimed at acquiring their land and
assimilating them into white culture, while abolishing their
own. Between 1782 and 1830 more than thirty treaties were
signed that affected the land holdings and lifestyle of the
Choctaw, ending with their removal in the 1830's.

We managed to hike another three miles before
finding a secluded spot to camp for the evening. I decided to
sleep in the open to enjoy the stars and night air. I lay in bed
watching the moon slowly rise, listening to the coyotes howl
in the distance.

A new day began and many more discoveries lay
ahead. We pushed hard and reached the old town site of
Rocky Springs just before noon. All that remains is a
graveyard and the echoes of the laughter and cries, the
dreams achieved and broken from two hundred years ago. I
wonder if the sound of the town's people laughing can still
be heard in space. How long does sound travel? We rested,
enjoying the warmth of the beautiful fall day.

We traveled another eleven miles by four, reaching
the site of Mangum Mound. The Magnum Mound was an
impressive sight; rising high above the Mississippi
landscape. The ancient people of the Plaquemine Culture
built the mound, a culture the Natchez Indians would follow
rather closely centuries later. As in most cultures, the chief

was highly regarded and his death was a time of great mourning. The burial observance lasted several days and included dancing, processions as well as several ceremonies. The chief's wife, servants, as well as any others who wanted to volunteer for the privilege, were sedated and ritually strangled as part of the ceremonies. I guess this ritual would provide great incentive for the servants to keep the chief healthy. Their bodies were then placed on special raised tombs and covered with branches and mud. They were left to sit and for several weeks. They were later removed to be stored in baskets in the temple. Eventually, the bones were buried in a platform in the temple or in the mound when it was expanded. The son of the dead chief's sister became the next ruler.

We continued on several miles before stopping again at a section of the original Trace. This section had two deep ruts worn more than fourteen feet deep by the heavy traffic. After the first became so deep, they moved the trail and wore another canyon into the soft delta soil. The Trace is worn deeply in certain areas because the soil is unusual.

During the last ice age, the deserts of western America were engaged in massive windstorms, and the wind blew the sand all the way to Mississippi and Louisiana. Large mountains or bluffs of sandy soil were left behind, much like snowdrifts. The mounds of soil, known as loess soil, were very loose, filled with pockets of air. Over the centuries they were covered with a thin layer of topsoil. The focused traffic along the Trace through the loess bluffs wore deep ruts into them, some as deep as forty-five feet.

We spent more time touring than we had expected and found ourselves a mile out of town as the sun began to set. We reached the town of Port Gibson in the last remnants of daylight, and found our way to the only hotel in town.

By the time the Civil War rolled around, Port Gibson was filled with graceful homes and grand churches. Control of the Mississippi River was crucial to the success of both sides, and the commercial town of Port Gibson was critical. On May 1, 1863, General Grant led 24,000 troops into battle against 8,000 Confederates in the Battle of Port Gibson.

According to legend, General Grant spared Port Gibson after defeating the Confederates saying that the town was "too beautiful to burn." The victory gave the Union a firm footing in Mississippi and was the first victory in the Vicksburg Campaign.

The next morning we passed by several of the large Victorian style mansions and talked with the local townspeople. The mansions stand as proud as they ever have, though their role in the society has changed. They are weathered and worn, and their large open yards are cluttered with smaller common houses. They still command respect, and I am sure when general Grant was here, they were an imposing sight.

As I started out of town a van pulled up. Inside a woman, smiling brightly, asked how far I might be traveling. She said she had seen me uptown with my backpack and knew I was a traveler. She couldn't stop then as the traffic was busy but since our path crossed again, she just had to say "hi." I leaned into the passenger side window for twenty minutes as we talked about religion and chasing dreams. As I bid her goodbye, she thanked me informing me that our meeting had given her a calm and renewed focus to chase one of her long time dreams.

Dodger's back pain was still very bad, but it was our last night on the old Natchez Trace. It looked like he would make it to town, but if the four days rest did not help; it might be the end of the trail for him. We spent our last night at the Coles Creek picnic area, sleeping on the picnic tables.

Dodger barely slept at all as the thought of dropping out haunted him.

The next morning we were up and hiking in the morning chill watching the sun slowly rise to warm the day. We had hiked only a few miles when we reached Mount Locust, the only stand along the Trace still in existence. I walked up the long row of steps to the front porch, which covered the whole front of the house. The porch is where many a traveler slept when stopping on the journey. We toured the old building, which is decorated as it was in the early 1800's with pewter plates on the small kitchen table and candles on the wall for light. The bedrooms were adorned with rope beds and a fireplace for warmth. Knowing we would be back to film the television show, we did not spend a lot of time.

Our last stop along the parkway was Emerald Mound. Thirty-five feet high, and covering eight acres it is the second largest Native American ceremonial mound in the United States. It was built and used from around 1250 A.D. to 1700 A.D. by the Natchez Indians. On top of the primary mound are two secondary mounds. Originally there were four or six secondary mounds located along the sides of the massive main mound. It was the main ceremonial mound center for the Natchez tribe at one time. Sometime before the La Salle Expedition of 1682, the Natchez abandoned the mound, shifting the main ceremonial center to the Grand Village/Fatherland site. There is no clue as to why they moved the site. The people of the tribe still gathered at the mound for religious and social events. The Emerald mound was used strictly for ceremonies, unlike many other mounds, which were also used as a burial site. The place is awesome and has a special energy about it.

We reached town, ending eleven weeks of hiking. We had taken only four days off in eleven weeks, covering over five hundred and sixty miles since our last day off. My focus was on preparing to film the television show, resting and reflecting on Mississippi.

I thought back to the many friendly people I met, to the inspiration and friendship I encountered. I thought of the swamps, the forest, the cotton fields of Mississippi. The rich history of the Natchez Trace had been an uplifting experience, a joyous journey back in time for me. I know that folks from my native Ohio traveled this route, floating their goods down the Ohio and Mississippi, selling them, and then walking back home. They had some benefits I did not have, such as streams that were safe to drink from and an abundance of game to hunt. They had the inns or stands for shelter. Of course I had benefits they did not have—better lightweight gear and a safer environment. The chance of being robbed or ambushed on the Trace now is miniscule. Tecumseh also traveled parts of this path. Tecumseh was one of the most brilliant Native American leaders of whom we have record. His vision, leadership ability, and passion are a credit to him and all Native Americans. I was thrilled to have walked a piece of the earth he had walked. Indeed, the Natchez Trace had been a remarkable section of my journey, one that I would not soon forget.

We walked along the busy streets of Natchez, staring down another brilliant sinking red sun. Natchez is the oldest town on the Mississippi River and we met Don Colliver, our producer, for dinner at the oldest building in Natchez, Kings Tavern. It was built around 1790 and legend says the old building is haunted.

In the 1930's during a restoration project, three skeletons were found behind a chimney. No one knows how long they had been there, but for years people have witnessed a young female walking around the building. Many believe the ghost to be that of the original owner's young mistress, Madeline. She has been known to turn water faucets on or knock jars off of shelves, and footsteps can often be heard when no one is walking around.

Other ghosts of Kings Tavern include a crying baby, heard even when there are no children on the premises, and a man who is often seen wearing a red hat. He has no face, he's just a figure and a red hat. After hearing the tales, I was glad that I was only to enjoy dinner, and not stay in the room for rent upstairs.

After a delightful dinner, I got my first view of the Mississippi River. I gazed out at Louisiana on the other side. I looked again in awe at the many old mansions; most built between 1790 and 1840. They seemed to be better kept than those in Port Gibson. The city has incredible character, a southern charm and timelessness about it.

Back at the hotel, I called Nina to learn she was not sure if she could make it, her workload was heavy. I had one sponsor, Wanderlust Gear. They supplied me with a tent, and I wanted to wear one of their T-shirts for the filming. It was mailed to Nina and she was supposed to bring it to me.

The next morning Don picked me up at the hotel at 7:30. John and Hans, who provide video and audio support for the filming, were with him. The show is called Radical Sabbatical, and profiles people who have given up the security of corporate America to chase personal dreams. Each show is thirty minutes long, and includes two profiles. After commercials, my fifteen minutes of fame would amount to about twelve minutes. To capture twelve minutes of film for the show we would shoot over six hours of film in three days.

The first morning was spent interviewing me. We interviewed for two and a half hours, sitting in a wooded area just off the Natchez Trace Parkway. We could only shoot while no cars were passing by, so as not to have their sound in the background of the audio.

Don headed back to town to get lunch and to pick up Dodger for the afternoon session, while John, Hans and I stayed in the field. When he returned, Nina was with them. She made it! What a pleasant surprise. Nina was transcribing my daily journal onto the internet for me, but I had not seen her since the Trail Days festival held in Damascus, Virginia in May. We had grown closer while I hiked—friends who shared a passion for hiking.

The afternoon was spent filming us as we hiked in different settings: up the road, back down the road; up the hill, back down the same hill; hike faster, hike slower; get a camera angle from the ground, let's shoot from a moving car. We all pitched in with ideas that would show what it was like to be hiking. Late in the day, we went back to Emerald Mound to set up a typical campsite and filmed camp scenes such as cooking, setting up the tent, going to bed, and watching another magnificent sunset from atop the mound. After the sunset, we all returned to Natchez. It was a long day, to say the least. I was amazed at the attention to detail that is paid to lighting, position of the sun, background noises, and a hundred other minor details. Nina and I went out to eat seafood for dinner, leaving Dodger and the crew to fend for themselves. We had a wonderful evening and during our conversation discovered we had much more in common than we thought. With a 5:00AM wake up the next day however, it was early to bed.

We were up before the sun and off to the campsite to setup for a sunrise in camp and more camp scenes. After that, we continued my interview and conducted an interview with Dodger. Then we went to Mount Locust, the old stand that we passed a few days prior. They filmed us interacting with the park ranger Eric Chamberlain, who was born in the house. The house was in his family from the day it was built in 1812 until about 1940 when the Park Service bought it. He shared several stories about the old place with us. We then filmed more footage of us hiking in various locations.

Sunday was a wrap up day and went quickly. We were finished by noon and it was time for everyone to go their separate ways. John and Hans back to New Orleans, and Don back to Los Angeles. Nina stuck around a while as Dodger decided he needed to take some time to let his ailing back heal. He was deeply depressed at the thought, but we both knew he needed the rest. We took him to the bus station and dropped him off. Just like that he was gone, on his way back to Oklahoma. He hoped to be able to rejoin me later in the fall, but I knew it was likely he would not hike with me again until I left Oklahoma in January. Nina and I spent the rest of the afternoon together and then she too was gone. We had grown very close in Natchez and hoped we would get the chance to see each other again.

I sat alone in the hotel room, coming down from the hectic weekend. I studied my maps of Louisiana to decide what my best route would be. As I sat there it dawned on me: I would hike across the Mississippi River Bridge alone.

Louisiana & Arkansas

I left the hotel at 9:30 and walked the three miles into downtown Natchez. I stopped to eat a good breakfast before walking to a local park at the river's bank where I took several pictures of the seemingly endless river. There wasn't much traffic on it as Natchez is a not nearly as important a shipping port as it once was. It was once the state capitol, and during the first half of the nineteenth century the town boomed as a major hub in the cotton industry. While cotton is still a major crop, Natchez is no longer needed to ship it. The city has endured and adapted however, creating a thriving tourism industry to fill the void.

I had stalled long enough-I needed to get across the river. I hiked another mile south until I reached the massive bridge that stands a hundred feet or more above the water. The traffic along the highway was very busy, this being the main route across the river. I was glad to see a large berm, giving me plenty of room to safely hike across. It took nearly twenty minutes to traverse the span, but soon enough I found myself standing in Louisiana, my sixth state. The roadway was lined with large American flags, in a show of patriotism. It was an impressive sight, but as I had seen so many times in the past, the flags were improperly displayed. They had no lights on them, and flag etiquette states to fly a flag after dark, it must have a light on it.

I had seen so many people and places in the past weeks displaying our flag improperly—flying them to tatters on their cars, or towns flying them along the streets. The thought and intentions were pure, but to a veteran such as myself, it is a sad reminder of how little we as a nation know about our flag and heritage.

I hiked on and passed The Sand Bar restaurant where Nina and I had enjoyed dinner a few nights before. I thought of her as I passed by, wondering if and when I might see her again. Hiking out of town, I left the noise of the constant flow of traffic behind. I hiked down the back road until nearly dark, and then found a wooded spot to pitch my tent. As I set it up I discovered that I had no tent pegs. I had left them at the campsite the other morning when we were filming. No tent pegs, I can deal with that, I thought. I found a good, sturdy stick and made some tent pegs. That got me through the night.

Late the next morning I reached the outskirts of Jonesville, Louisiana, where I crossed the Black River, a much scarier crossing than the Mississippi. This bridge was not as long, nor as high, but as I peered across, it sure looked awfully narrow. I stared at it for several minutes but it didn't get any bigger. I finally looked up and said, "Lord, I'm in your hands on this one," and started across. Fortunately, the traffic was light and the cars coming by shared what little road there was with me. It was the scariest bridge I had crossed.

Safely across the bridge and in town, I stopped at the hardware store in search of tent pegs. All they carried were very large heavy stakes for a canopy or something. They were much too heavy for my purpose so I bought some lightweight aluminum rods. I hoped they were strong enough, but it didn't matter, as they were my best option at the moment.

In town, a historical marker informed me that the Spanish explorer Hernando DeSoto fought his last battle nearby. DeSoto had come to America, not in search of gold, but to find a trade route to China and to colonize America for Spain. He arrived in 1538 and traveled much of the North American interior. In 1541, he became the first white man to see the Mississippi River.

The full impact he and his army had on the natives and the continent would not be understood for centuries. The natives had never seen horses ridden before nor had they ever encountered dogs as vicious as those DeSoto brought with him. DeSoto and his men had enslaved Indians for years in Mexico and South America, and the North American Indians, with their primitive weapons, were no match either. They were chained and forced to harvest and carry food for DeSoto's army. The women and children were raped and abused, and the world's diseases were inflicted upon all of them.

He left the area in search of his elusive route, but had greatly miscalculated the size of the continent and returned in the fall of 1541. He died on May 21st 1542, before he could establish a colony.

In the decade that followed his journey, the landscape changed drastically as entire villages were abandoned and perished—poisoned with European diseases from which they had no immunity. DeSoto set the tone for European sentiments towards the natives in the later centuries. They were red devils and undeserving of friendship and civil treatment.

The day began to heat up as I headed out of town. Trees in this part of Louisiana are scarce; fields dominate the landscape. I hiked along with the heat reflecting off the pavement making it even hotter for me. Several hours later I happened across a large shade tree beside the road with a house sitting seventy yards or so behind it. I stopped to rest. I sat, drinking water and looking at my map when the owner came up from behind. He was curious why I was there, sitting in his yard. He introduced himself as Mr. Tip Netherland. After our introductions he invited me in for coffee and I quickly accepted the offer. We enjoyed a pleasant conversation for almost an hour. All good things must end, and soon enough I was back on my way, grateful for the friendship and hospitality.

I walked into a wooded area as dusk drew near. I thought to myself what a beautiful place to camp. The little island of forest was beautiful, I had found home for the night. I walked a little deeper and noticed the Tupelo and Cypress tress growing, a sure sign of a swamp. I had my equipment laying about the ground and had just begun to set up my tent when the mosquitoes found me. I picked up the pace, trying to set my tent up as quickly as I could. I pushed my new tent stakes into the dry hard ground and the bent one after another. They bent, but I got them deep enough into the ground to hold the tent for tonight.

I had to cook dinner while wearing my long sleeve shirt and pants to protect me from the bugs. I quickly gobbled down my Lipton noodle dinner and climbed into the safety of my tent. The still night air was interrupted off and on by several owls hooting in the distant. I was alone, and the lullaby the forest sang gave me the feeling it knew I was alone as well. I eventually fell asleep gazing at the stars above.

My morning walk took me along a fence line. There was a group of about ten songbirds sitting on the fence, watching me. When I got close to them they flew several feet down the fence then stopped to watch me approach again. We played this way for an eighth of a mile and I could not help but laugh at the silly, curious birds. I was feeling better, the incident lifted my spirits.

Shortly after, a school bus passed me, the driver waved, and she looked back as she passed. Twenty minutes later a truck pulled up. It was the bus driver and her sister, Rose and Michelle Hamilton, along with their children. Much like the birds, they were curious about where I had come from and where I was heading. Despite warnings from their mother that I might be a vagrant, they came to visit. During our conversation they asked if I needed anything. "A little water would be a blessing," I replied. They invited me to their house but we decided it would be better if they came back with water. They left and fifteen minutes later returned with a gallon of water. I have found it a most humbling experience that people will take time from their busy day to help an old hiker. Thank you so much, Michelle and Rose.

I reached the small town of Aimwell at about 10:00 where I met Rocky Ford in his yard. We talked a spell and he gave me directions to the town of Olla using back roads. I sat in his yard to enjoy a long-overdue breakfast before shouldering my pack again. Just around the corner was the post office. I had a few things to mail and stopped in to meet the postmaster, a 72-year-old lady whose name I do not recall. She was a joy. She helped me package my items and made me some coffee inviting me to stay and chat also. As I prepared to leave, she gave me a lemon she had grown herself to take with me. What a friendly little town is Aimwell.

After another three miles I reached the crossroad that Mr. Ford told me about—the crossroad where I left the pavement and headed across the Louisiana woods on a back road. The next eight miles were through private land owned by paper companies. They lease the land to hunting clubs who then sublet it to individuals. You get your square of land, build a tree stand, and then you're ready for the big hunt. And when you get your square, well you just have to post it so anyone who might come near knows that this here square of prime huntin' soil is yours.

Every fifty yards was a new "No Trespassing" sign, identifying the individual who has purchased the rights to hunt their little plot of land; every fifty yards for eight miles. Much of the land had been clear-cut, and I again had little protection from the hot sun. I saw several buzzards, a hawk, a crane and a squirrel, but despite the wildlife the land seemed sad, like a beaten child. I felt no joy in the ground.

I reached the town of Olla and the hotel around five as the sun was setting. I checked into the room and then quickly changed into my cleanest dirty shirt, all set to go to dinner. The twenty-eight mile day had taken a toll on me, and my body was already stiff. I hobbled the quarter mile to the closest restaurant, a local pizza shop.

After dinner I returned to take a well-deserved shower. I had hiked over seventy miles in three days and had not enjoyed a shower since leaving Natchez. I called Nina to learn that she would be passing through the area on the weekend, on her way to hike in Arkansas with a friend. We both wanted to see each other again and so we made plans for Friday night. I went to sleep with a happy beat in my heart.

I was still very stiff when I awoke the next morning, the night's sleep doing little to counter the effects of the many miles I had hiked the past few days. This day looked to be no easier as I planned to hike twenty-two more miles. The morning hike led me past a cow pasture. Cows are curious creatures, and will generally follow whatever the first one does. If she is frightened and runs, they will all run, not knowing why, just blindly following the one who moved first. The first one this morning came running to me; soon they were all crowding the fence line to get a glimpse. There were several small stands of trees between the fence and me, so I would pass in and out of view. The entire herd ran down the fence line stopping at every viewpoint, muscling into position to catch another glimpse.

Later in the day I crossed a bridge under repair and spent some time chatting with the four guys working there. They were excited about my journey, but told me to be careful. They informed me there were some crazy folks living in the area. It seems everywhere I have been people think they have the only wild and boisterous people in the country. Little do they realize the land is filled with them. Even so, I have found them all to be friendly and curious.

I was getting low on water later that day. I passed a house with a woman out in front and decided to stop. I asked if she might be able to give me some water. She came off the porch and led me around back to the pump to get water from her spring.

"This is where the good water is," she informed me.

It was fine water indeed. I drank a quart and then filled my bottles with enough to get me to my next stop, the small town of Sikes.

When I arrived, I found the only two businesses in town: a little restaurant, and a small general store. The restaurant named Kim's Country Kitchen was a small stand run out of a trailer with some seats outside. Kim Stewart owns and operates the place, and we talked of my great journey while I ordered a cheeseburger and fries. I then went next door to get a coke, so as to patronize everyone in town. Upon returning, Kim asked the usual questions and insisted that she give me my meal. I was again humbled by the kindness and generosity of a person I had known for only ten minutes, and will probably never see again. Your kindness will long be remembered, Kim.

After dinner, I walked to the house of Pastor Bill Mills to see if I could pitch my tent in the churchyard. I met all of Pastor Mills' family, except Pastor Mills. His wife, daughter and son were home; he was out on church duties. We chatted for half an hour before I went on to the churchyard with their blessings.

My tent was wet from the night's heavy dew as I packed it the next morning. I walked back to the general store for a cup of coffee and a sausage biscuit or two where I chatted with the proprietor and a few morning regulars. I asked about a shortcut to Jonesboro, where I was to meet Nina.

"Well, go up the road a piece till ya see Catfish House Road. That is the magic shortcut. It is an old dirt road; ya won't see anything but loggin' trucks out that way, so be careful out there," was the advice given to me collectively from the group.

I was on my way out of town at 7:15, stopping briefly to talk with some high school students waiting for the school bus. Bidding them a good day, I walked just over a mile and a half when I found Catfish House road, just as I had been told. The next five miles were spent walking alone down this lonely old road. There was not even a breeze and I had my fleece top off by eight.

Along the quiet dirt road I spotted two buzzards sitting in a dead tree. They were straight in front of me and I kept my eye on them, walking ever closer. The one on the right spread his wings to dry in the morning sun, and a few seconds later the other one followed suit. They were kings of the world atop their perch, and I was a mere peasant muddling along on the ground below. I felt fortunate to be able to take some pictures of them.

The land in northern Louisiana is not perfectly flat, as I had imagined. It has some rolling hills—well, almost hills. The forest is dominated by pine and the roads by logging trucks. In Ohio, the coal trucks run. In Louisiana, timber rules. It is an important crop that provides a livelihood for many folks in the area. Even though the site of clear-cut fields hurts me deeply, I fully realize we all love our wood products.

I continued down the rough dirt road as several logging trucks rumbled past me. Eventually a truck loaded with pine trees stopped and the driver asked me where I was bound, offered me a ride, then wished me well. I had been warned to be wary of careless truckers, but every one that passed me did so with caution and shared the road with me. Don't get me wrong, I got off the road when they came by (that is how I shared the road), but they always moved over when they could.

Past Catfish Road I found another very inviting front yard to rest in. I sat with my back to the house and took off my shoes to let my feet breathe a bit. I sat oblivious to the world around me; unaware of the danger I was in. The attack came silently, from behind. I never saw it coming. The creature lunged onto me, licking and assaulting me with his soft cuddly paws. Indeed, I was in the yard of a puppy—a very playful puppy at that.

I was a big chew toy to him. Ahhh, was he ever lovable. He wanted to chew my socks, my shoes, my pack, and me. He was relentless in his pursuit of play, and I sat laughing at him for some time. When I got ready to leave, he wanted to become a hiking puppy. I had to yell at him to get him to go home.

Early that afternoon, I reached Jonesville and got cleaned up, did some laundry and caught up on my email while waiting for Nina to arrive. I spoke with Dodger and he reported to me that he was feeling no better. I would continue to hike alone. He mentioned coming to get me for Thanksgiving, to spend the holiday with his family.

Nina arrived around eight and we both were radiant with joy at seeing each other again. We talked the night away like two kids at a slumber party.

The next morning we went to breakfast together, then she drove on to Arkansas and the Ouachita Trail, and I back to the roadways bustling with logging trucks, and slaughtered forests. She would hike for a week, then pass my way again, and we planned to meet once more somewhere in Arkansas.

As I hiked through Bienville Parish I came very close to the highest point in Louisiana: Mount Driskill, which stands at 535 feet above sea level. Bienville Parish is also famous for being the end of the line for Bonnie Parker and Clyde Barrow. They met early in 1930 when Bonnie was nineteen, and married to an imprisoned murderer. Clyde was twenty-one. They were believed responsible for thirteen murders as well as numerous robberies since. Henderson Jordan, the sheriff of Bienville Parish, had secretly met an Arcadian man who was desperate. He was plying for fair treatment of his son Henry Methvin, who had been associated with Bonnie and Clyde. Henry told the sheriff Bonnie and Clyde were to rob the bank in Gibsland on May 25, and they could be found in an abandoned house outside of Sailes. Along with Texas Ranger Frank Hammer and several other law enforcement officers, they set up an ambush on Highway 154, a desolate dirt road leading to the abandoned house.

As Bonnie and Clyde reached the ambush, Sheriff Jordan stepped into the road ordering them out of the car with their hands up. Never ones to give up, they both reached for their weapons, Clyde an automatic rifle lying on the floor and Bonnie for the sawed-off shotgun she was never without. Neither of them got off a shot. The officers didn't hesitate to open fire when they did not immediately cooperate. The spray of gunfire cut the car and Bonnie and Clyde to pieces. Both were hit with over thirty-five shots, and the car had more than seventy-five rounds in it.

The next day was cloudy and rain looked immanent, but I was pushing hard to reach the Arkansas line to meet Dodger for Thanksgiving. A few miles north of Interstate 20, I passed an elderly gentleman working in his driveway. He asked where I might be bound, and as always I told my tale of adventure. We continued to chat and I could see his eyes and smile growing wider. As we parted he told me "I am so glad to have met you, hope you stay dry."

I hadn't hiked but a mile or so when the skies opened up. I quickly donned my pack cover and raincoat, and then continued north. Soon a car pulled up next to me. It was the gentleman I had spoken with earlier.

He yelled through the rain, "Come get in, get out of this weather."

I replied, "I am OK, I have equipment for this weather."

He then retorted, "No It's OK, it's me the old man," as if I wouldn't remember him from thirty minutes earlier.

I again assured him I would be fine, despite the heavy rain.

He pleaded one last time, "I'll fix ya some dinner."

Normally that would have been all it took, but I had been looking forward to a good walk in the rain for some time, and really needed to reach Arkansas, so I reluctantly declined again. He grudgingly went home without me. I probably should have taken the offer. As he drove away, I walked on just energized with the vigor he had.

As I hiked along on my last day in Louisiana, I reflected on my time in the state. Oil and timber rule the northern half of Louisiana. It is not the most beautiful place; it is a working man's place. It is also home to some of the kindest, warmest people I have had the pleasure of meeting. It has its own special charm and her people have shown me time and again that America is a land of compassionate people.

I reached a small convenience store and was preparing to call Dodger when a car pulled up to the phone. I was in no hurry and asked the gentleman if he needed the phone. He replied no, and introduced himself as Paul Latta. He just wanted to chat with me. He had seen me walking for a few days, and was curious as to why I was not hitchhiking and where I was headed. We talked for several minutes. He said if he wasn't so old he would join me and then gave me five dollars to buy my lunch with, yet another testimony to the kindness of people.

Paul drove off and I called Dodger. The plan was for him to pick me up the next day in Magnolia. He then asked, "Want me to come tonight?" I thought what the heck, it would cut his drive in half and it sure would be good to see him. I told him I would wait for him four miles into Arkansas. It would be a long six-hour drive for him, so we should meet around sunset.

As I hiked through town I was stopped again to be questioned, this time by four young kids. They were sure I was going to be in the Guinness Book of World Records. I pushed on to reach Arkansas, and reached mile marker four around 4:30. I had a cheese sandwich and listened to a great classic country radio station on my beloved Coby radio as I waited for Dodger. I was just sitting on the side of the road, minding my own business. There were several houses nearby, and I really looked out of place, but I knew Dodger would be there soon. As the sun set, a man who lived across the street stopped to see if I was OK. I told him I was waiting for a friend.

Soon it was dark and quickly turning cold. Still no
Dodger. A little later the Rottweiler down the street
found me and approached me, barking incessantly. I
shined my flashlight at him and he retreated.

6:30, and still no Dodger. I began to get cold
sitting in the open air. At 6:55, I ducked behind a line of
trees to pitch my tent and was soon warm in my sleeping
bag. A few minutes later, the Rottweiler was back,
barking at my tent. I shined the light at him through the
tent and he again ran off. He must have been pretty
confused. He returned for a third time; again the light
drove him back.

I gave up on Dodger and was falling in and out of
sleep when I awoke to Dodger screaming, "Daniel Lee
Rogers, where the Hell are you?"

I quickly replied, " WOHOOOO DODGER" as I
bumbled around in my dark tent trying to find my light
and get out to find him.

The dog was barking at his feet as he walked up
and down the road. Dodger had made it to the area
around 6:30 but in the darkness we somehow missed
each other. He spent four hours searching for me and
was about to give up as well. His persistence paid off
and we were reunited.

I quickly tore down my tent and jumped into his
car. We drove into Magnolia to get a room. I was quite
hungry and was glad to see an all night diner. After the
late dinner, we went back to the room to catch up on life.

The next morning, Dodger drove me back to mile
point four and I hiked the fourteen miles into Magnolia.
He was waiting for me there to take me to his house for a
well-deserved Thanksgiving break. I spent two days

with Dodger and his parents, Leon and Mary. On Friday
night, Dodger drove me to Texarkana, Arkansas to meet
Nina on her way south.

The next morning Dodger was up and gone early,
so Waterfall and I went to breakfast and then set out to
explore some of Arkansas. We went to historic Old
Washington State Park, a restored town from the early
1800s. We made candles and toured an old house, seeing
how the people lived back then. It had old rope beds,
and the kitchen was separate from the main house. Often
times, the kitchen would be a separate building to protect
the main house from danger of fire.

Our next stop was the town of Stamps, Arkansas.
Nina's father, Hugh, spent some of his childhood there.
We tried to find the house where he had lived. We
stopped in front of a house that Nina believed should be
the one he lived in from the directions her Aunt had
given. There was a gentleman in the yard, so we pulled
into the driveway. Here we met Eddie and Josie Ann
Hester. When we told Eddie why we stopped, he was
excited to meet us. He invited us in, and gave us a tour
of the house. We enjoyed a drink with him and his wife
while discussing local history. Josie then walked with us
back to the old high school to show us the sidewalk with
the names of each graduating class from 1930 to 1937
etched into the pavement. They invited us to stay for
dinner, but we declined, wanting to spend the last of our
time together alone.

We headed on to Magnolia, Arkansas where I
would resume my walk the next morning. As we sat at a
local diner enjoying dinner, Tara, our waitress, asked us
in her strong southern accent, "Where y'all from?"

We told her, and Nina mentioned my adventure. We soon had four employees at the table asking questions and enjoying hearing tales of the journey.

When I left Ohio, I had left to hike for me. As I traveled farther and farther along, I began to realize that I had an impact on the lives of so many, as they had me. The hike was not just about me seeing America; it was a chance to bring a smile to people, to share my dream and to allow them to live vicariously through me. What a great feeling.

The next morning, I was up and off to breakfast with Nina, and then I went back to my hotel room to pack up. After a see-you-soon kiss, I was hiking under magnificent blue skies in southwest Arkansas. I was soon out of town and hiking alone along route 82, daydreaming of Nina as well as the road ahead. The pavement was very rough, and by the time I reached Stamps, my feet were tender and sore.

As I continued on I noticed a change in the landscape. I was out of the southern pine forest, and the forested areas I passed were a mixture of hardwood with stands of intermixed pine. Oil wells dotted the landscape, slowly pumping that black gold from the ground. Another large part of the landscape is pasture—large pastures with hundreds of heads of cattle in them. I also saw more blackbirds on that day than any day I can recall. I passed several flocks with anywhere from one hundred to one thousand in each. That is a lot of blackbirds.

I was only about four miles out of Stamps when it started to sprinkle. My blue skies had gone south with Nina, I guess. As I stopped to put my pack cover on I noticed a man up the road taking a sign in off the highway, saving it from the approaching rain. It was the daily special sign for the Kuntry Kitchen. I was quickly hiking again and passed by the restaurant when the man reappeared with a plate of cookies.

He stopped me and asked, "'Pardon me sir, would you like some cookies? A gift from the Kuntry Kitchen!"

I could have cried. The intense gratitude that wells up inside when a person you have never seen before, and will probably never see again, displays that kind of fellowship towards another is just overwhelming. And cookies are my friend, to boot. Wow. We spoke briefly, before he disappeared as quickly as he came.

I ate a few and then secured the rest into a Ziploc to protect them from what was beginning to look like a pretty good storm. The western horizon was turning black and soon I could see the lightning and hear the thunder across the flat land. As I stared at the horizon, I noticed a mountain range in the distance. It was not very tall, but it was good to see a mountain again, even a little one. I watched as the storm grew ever closer with bolt after bolt of lightening crashing to the ground ever closer to me. When the storm finally reached me, it raged with a fury I had not seen since the Indian mounds in Mississippi. This time I did not have the protection of my tent, and the rain stung my face and the wind blew hard against me as I walked into it. My vision was obscured as my glasses were smudged with raindrops. A car stopped and offered me refuge, but I was managing to stay dry in my rain gear. I had carried it for so long; it felt good to use it.

The rain continued to come down in wave after wave and the fields around me were quickly saturated.

After twenty-five minutes or so, the worst of it passed by and the blue skies remerged from beyond, allowing the sun to peek through. My shoes and socks were drenched, as well as my pants, but I was warm and happy. I trudged on, enjoying the many smells that filled the air: the smell of life anew, the smell of promise, and of success. As the day warmed again, the fog and mist rose from the wet ground, giving an eerie feeling to the landscape.

As the day lingered on, the temperatures dropped and I decided to make it to the edge of Texarkana where I was sure I had seen a hotel when Dodger and I had driven through. As dusk fell, I found myself very low on water and determined I would find the hotel I remembered. The road had a very wide berm and was fairly safe to night-hike on, but I was not crazy about the idea. I trudged on through twilight and soon I was hiking in the dark with my headlamp on. I always hike facing traffic so I can see them and know they would be able to see my small headlight. I finally realized the hotel I sought did not exist.

Shortly after six, I saw a sign for a Bed & Breakfast. I stopped in and met Sandra & Jeral Willard. They were not open yet, but had a sign out front. When I explained my situation to them, they were kind enough to give me a spot in the shed out back. They invited me in to use their kitchen and take a shower. We had a wonderful visit, and I was very appreciative of their hospitality.

The weather forecast the next morning was not good, so I was up and gone early trying to make it into town before the cold winter storm hit the area. I made it into Texarkana by noon, high and dry. Not long after I arrived, the rains started again. It was a cold rain that didn't let up all that afternoon and into the next day. Road walking is very different from wilderness hiking. On the road, there are no trees to absorb the wind and rain. When it rains, you face the full force of the storm as well as the additional inflicted splashing from the cars and trucks passing by. I decided not to venture out into it, took the next day off, and watched TV to pass the time. I only ventured out long enough to eat, and then back to the luxury and safety of the hotel.

I was awake early and feeling restless, but the rain has not stopped in over forty hours and the temperature had dropped as well. I went out to get a feel for just how bad it really was and decided to head out, despite not having any good winter gear with me. The rain was not nearly as heavy, and my goal was to do just seventeen miles to the next town and another warm hotel. If something bad should happen, I had my tent and cold weather sleeping bag.

I was out of the hotel at nine-thirty, headed up the street to McDonald's for breakfast. At 10:00 A.M., I was on my way out of Texarkana in the slow drizzle. Soon the rain picked up in intensity and I briefly considered stopping before I got past all of the hotels, but choose to continue on. I slogged along, my feet wet already and my hood pulled down to protect my face. I was not waving to cars as they passed by as I normally did. I was in a good mood, but I rarely lifted my head to look at the drivers in the cars. The rain was coming from the southwest, pounding me on my back left side. My left hand was cold, as I did not have my fleece gloves on, just my rainproof over-gloves. After about five miles, I stopped to put on my fleece top and fleece gloves. The rain continued and so did I.

The high temperature reached only thirty-five degrees, and the wind was biting. About 1:00 P.M., I noticed that my pants had somehow gotten wet—soaking wet. The lightweight rain jacket I had was not very long, and the bottom of my shirt had become exposed to the weather. The rain wicked down the tucked-in shirt and got my short pants under my rain pants wet. I didn't notice it until I began to get cold. I untucked my shirt and the flow of cold water stopped. Without the steady stream of cold water, my body was able to produce enough heat to keep me warm despite being wet. The rain eventually turned to ice and snow. I trudged on with the wind-driven ice stinging my cheeks. I certainly missed my beard.

I reached the edge of Ashdown around three and stopped at McDonald's for a hot cup of coffee and to get out of the weather a bit. Twenty minutes later I was hiking again, and reached a small hotel just before four. It was a demanding day, but I was glad to get the miles behind me. It certainly felt good to get a hot shower and put my driest clothes on. After dinner, I called Nina and we talked the night away.

I awoke to the phone ringing; it was Nina calling to tell me the sad news of the passing of George Harrison. Time waits for no man, which was one of the biggest reasons I was there in the first place. The idea of hiking America had occupied my mind the past few years, and I could no longer stand the thought of never doing it. I was fortunate to be in a position to be able to chase the dream and grateful to have had the courage to go.

I dressed slowly; thinking of all that George Harrison gave to the world. I took forever to get out of town, energy seemingly hard to come by. I hiked all day and reached the small town of Foreman, Arkansas late in the afternoon. This small forgotten town of 1,100 people is the birthplace of country singer Tracey Lawrence. I stopped briefly in town to get food for dinner and then headed west, Oklahoma bound.

On my way out of town, I passed two young girls on the sidewalk, along with their mother and baby sister standing in the yard. They were very curious, as I am sure they had never seen a guy with a pack and hiking poles pass by their front yard before. The asked a hundred questions and wanted to try my hiking poles. I let both of them try my hiking poles, they could not have been more proud. We talked and played for nearly fifteen minutes before I bid them farewell and disappeared like an old cowboy into the sinking sunset.

The girls brought a smile to my face. It was good to see kids who are so curious, who like to learn and enjoy people. The sunset was enjoyable as there was not a cloud to be found. As a matter of fact, I had not seen a cloud all day. As day turned to night, I watched the moon rising behind me, full and magnificent. It was the last day of November and the month's second full moon—a rare blue moon. It was a welcome sight as it lit up the road and made my night hike much more enjoyable. I only turned my headlamp on when a car approached, which was rare. I reached the Oklahoma line right at 6:00 P.M. and then found a spot in the woods to pitch my tent.

I was awakened around 3:00 A.M. to the song of coyotes. What a magical song it is, eerie and romantic. Its lonely tone reverberates across the land letting all of the creatures of the night world know that they are not alone. I woke for good at 6:30, lying in my tent in the cold morning air. It was good to be in my tent again, sleeping on the ground. As I stuffed my wet tent into its stuff sack, I gazed at the eastern sky painted with feathery clouds of brilliant red. I had many a mile to hike, and couldn't wait for the sun to warm the air. My gloves, still damp from the rain two days before, coupled with the cold morning air, made for very cold hands.

I was back in Choctaw country, on the lands that had become their home when they were removed from Mississippi in the 1830's. I passed a historical marker that spoke of a Choctaw Chief that was buried nearby. When he arrived, he started a ranch and used slave labor to run it. I found this bit of history a bizarre twist; a man who had just been treated so wrongly, deported from his own land, would own slaves. I pondered that reality as I hiked along.

I reached Millerton and the sight of the Wheelock Mission. Reverend Alfred Wright and his wife Harriet established it in 1832 for the Choctaw Nation. The stone church, which was built in 1846, is the oldest standing church in Oklahoma. It was also used as a school for the Choctaw peoples until 1955.

The day turned cooler and it started to rain, so when I found Dodger at the entrance to the Raymond Gary State Park I decided to get out of the weather. We were about ten miles away from the sight of Fort Towson, and I would not get to see it on the hike, so we spent the afternoon touring the old facility.

When we arrived, an elderly gentleman we caught napping in his chair greeted us. Rainy Mondays in December can be slow for tourism. He was most helpful, however, and toured us through the site. The original fort was built in 1824 and was on the cutting edge of the frontier. The Red River, just about ten miles south, was then the Mexican border. The soldiers regulated trade between the white settlers and Indians and maintained peace.

The original fort was burned in 1829 and rebuilt in 1830 after the Treaty of Dancing Rabbit Creek. This treaty provided for the removal of the Choctaw people to Oklahoma, and the fort was built to protect them. The fort was a very busy place as more than twelve thousand Choctaws moved into the area. With construction of forts further west and settlement of hostilities with Mexico, Fort Towson's role became less important. The last major event that occurred there was the surrender of General Stand Watie nearby. It was the last organized resistance of the Civil War. It was a special place, and I felt fortunate to be able to spend some time on the hallowed ground.

The next morning, my last before I returned east to take a break over the winter, was again cold and wet. I trekked on alone, in no great hurry. It was a day of reflection for me. I thought back to the many days and experiences of the journey: to the horse Dodger found and the Mays Brothers in Kentucky; to Old Man's Cave and the Buckeye Trail in Ohio; to the visit with my Aunt and the magnificent history of the Natchez Trace; to the opportunity to film for a national TV show in Natchez; to losing Dodger and meeting Waterfall; to the thunderstorm in Mississippi and the freezing rain in Texarkana.

I reached Dodger at the site of the Rose Hill Plantation, which was the home of Colonel Robert M. Jones, the wealthiest Choctaw. He owned five hundred

slaves. He was also the delegate from the Choctaw
Nation to the Confederate Congress at Richmond,
Virginia.

This was the end of the line for now, but I would
return in February to resume the hike. I would soon be
back east, spending time with Nina and my family over
the holidays. But on this last day, I had a big grin on my
face. I was overrun with emotion; filled with joy and
sadness, incredible memories and sweet dreams, friends
and acquaintances, pain and elation. I looked to the
partly cloudy sky, looked around at the Oklahoma
landscape-- rugged with open fields and broken sections
of trees. I was happy to be there, happy to have achieved
the first section of this magnificent journey, which
included so many emotions, so many beautiful sights, so
many interesting people, and so much history.

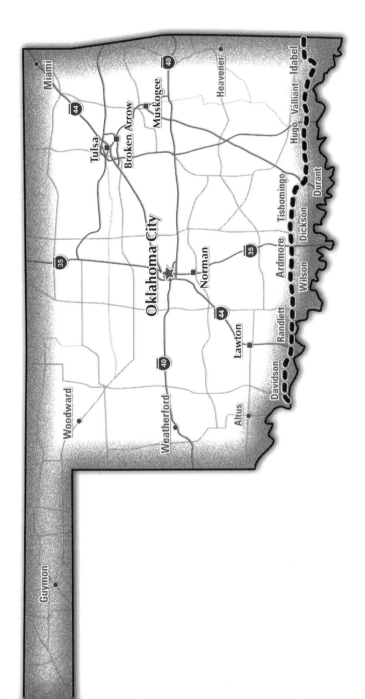

Oklahoma

Brooks woke me at 6:00 AM and we were soon on the road. I watched the sun rise over the Dallas skyline while I thought of my girlfriend Nina, who I had left in Louisiana. With the winter's break over, it was time to resume hiking, to get out and see more of the America I so deeply loved.

We arrived in Hugo, Oklahoma, at 9:30 and Brooks dropped me off at the historical marker where I left off last December. I hiked the last mile to the edge of town and the Holiday Motel parking lot where Brooks was waiting. It was a cool beautiful morning with perfect blue skies above. I wore my fleece hat and gloves along with my long pants and fleece top, as Brooks and I hiked together through Hugo. We hiked and talked, enjoying our first hike together since hiking into Bland, Virginia, together on the Appalachian Trail in 1999.

Dodger and his parents, Leon and Mary, found us at 11:45. It was good to see them again. We all talked for a while as Dodger double-checked his gear. Soon the time arrived to say goodbye and hike. Brooks got in the car with Dodger's parents, catching a ride back to his car, and Dodger joined me. Ahh, it was good to see Dodger.

We hiked about eight miles, watching several hawks fly above us. That afternoon we arrived in Soper, Oklahoma. We were both hungry, so we decided to stop at the Soper Cafe. The waitress delivered our order to the kitchen and then returned.

"Pardon me, but are you guys homeless?"

We chuckled and reassured her we were not, and explained the journey to her. She left only to return again in a few minutes.

"Your meal is on Karen, the owner. Your money is no good here, Karen says anyone walking all that way deserves a free meal!"

While we sat enjoying our cheeseburger and fries, Dave and Jean Liles, who were sitting at the next table could not help but to quiz us also.

Finally Dave asked, "Where ya'all gonna spend the night?"

Dodger replied, "down a few miles by Muddy Boggy Creek."

Dave then invited us to stay at his hunting cabin, which was located very close to the river. He assured us it was open, gave us directions and wished us well. Soon our waitress returned with a brown paper bag and informed us it had food for later tonight, compliments of the house.

We headed out of Soper around 4:00 grinning at our good fortune. We reached the little blue cabin about an hour later, finding a fireplace and two beds complete with mattresses inside. It was to be quite cold, so I did not hesitate to bring firewood from the pile out back and build a fire to warm the building. We were both still full from our late lunch and decided to save the very large ham and cheese sandwiches we found in our gift bag for breakfast.

The cabin sat on the property of the local hunting club, and we had not been there long before a club member stopped by to see who was wandering around.

He informed us, "My friend Junior saw a couple a guys, thought they were with me. Told me one of 'em was walkin' on crutches." He was obviously confused by my hiking poles.

We had a nice conversation about the local area but soon he was on his way. Dodger and I walked outside to carry in the last of the firewood. Dodger grabbed a load of wood and headed in, but I was entranced by the starry night above. I stood staring up at my old friend Orion the hunter, who was standing guard over the cold southern winter sky. Once inside and settled down for a good night of sleep, we could hear the coyotes howling in the stillness of the Oklahoma woods. It felt good to be back on the road, good to have the coyotes singing me to sleep again.

We hiked nearly twenty uneventful miles the following day, uneventful that is, except for the last few miles. The last miles were filled with thousands of starlings coming in to roost for the evening. I watched as flock after flock blackened the sky, all looking for a place to roost for the night. I had certainly never seen so many birds in all my life. Amazingly enough however, this was just a trickle of birds compared to the millions of passenger pigeons that dominated the countryside more than a century ago. Our goal was not to camp underneath them.

The next day we hiked another twenty miles, reaching the town of Durant and a hotel in time to watch the Superbowl. It was not a good idea to start off hiking so many miles each day. Our bodies were not in the same rough and ready shape as they were only weeks before. I lay in the bed watching the game with my body in full rebellion over the pain I had caused it. My left foot was swollen, and both calves and thighs sore. I had managed to blister the two smallest toes and the ball on my left foot. My right Achilles tendon was sore from rubbing back and forth in my shoe. I was sure that if I just kept on hiking, it would be ok, that sooner or later my body would get used to it again.

The next morning my blistered feet were still very tender and Dodger was in no better shape. While packing up, I heard on my radio that a winter storm was forecast for the next day, and just to keep things interesting, three escaped convicts were in the area. Armed with that information it was an easy decision to make it a short day and to take the next day off.

We called Dodger's parents and they agreed to meet us later in the day. We set out from the hotel and hobbled along on a cool cloudy morning. The six miles proved to be all my feet wanted for the day and I was glad to see the road sign announcing our arrival in Silo. We stopped at the Silo General Store, which appeared to be closed, but the curtain was slightly opened. I peered into the dark store from the front window to see a smiling face staring back at me from the couch inside. A moment later Betty opened the door and welcomed us inside.

"Well hello there, I am open! Business is usually pretty slow in the afternoon here, so that is when I take my nap."

Inside, the store was decorated with several original paintings. The seventy-one year old Choctaw native had painted them all. She made me a cup of coffee as Dodger got himself a Coke. She then pulled down her latest painting, a captivating portrait of a young Indian woman. We continued our visit with Betty until Dodger's parents arrived, at which time we hobbled in to the car and on our way to the comfort of the Ham household.

After a day of rest, Leon & Mary dropped us off at Betty's store. We went in to say good-bye to Betty. She had been busy since we had last seen her, and presented both of us with scarves she had made. She figured with the cold weather we might need them.

It was cold and windy outside, and I was bundled up with all the clothing I had. We hadn't gone very far when the snow resumed—not big soft flakes, but more of a windy, spitting, wet snow. The Oklahoma countryside is open and rarely were there trees to protect us from the wind. As we hiked along, a car came at us and stopped maybe forty yards in front of us. A man stepped out and approached us. It was a state policeman in an unmarked car, responding to a call about the missing convicts. He knew we were not the suspects, but stopped to make sure we were aware of their escape. Certain that he was curious as to why we were there, we told him about the adventure. He wished us luck and we wished him likewise.

That afternoon, we made it to the ruins of Fort Washita, built by the Union in 1842, and destroyed in 1861 by confederate soldiers from Texas. Legend has it that the ghost of Aunt Jane, who was murdered there, still haunts the site.

The Chickasaw took over the property after the Civil War as part of their treaty settlement. Charles Colbert moved in and rebuilt the barracks, making it a home for his family and their thirty-two dogs. Legend says that the first night in the house, all thirty-two of the dogs ran away. The next day he found them all, and brought them back only to have them run away again. Evidently this was all he needed to convince him he shouldn't live there and they moved out. Was it Aunt Jane?

Dodger and I hoped to spend the evening camped there, but camping was not normally permitted at the historical state park. The ranger told us we were in luck, however, as there was a big mountain man rendezvous that weekend. There were two men already camped nearby and we should have no problem joining them.

We hiked the half-mile to their campsite finding the two men, Mike and Doug, standing around their campfire, a homemade wooden tripod perched above it and a pot of cowboy coffee brewing, their white canvas tent in the background. They both wore grey beards and moccasins, and a knife strapped to their side. Mike was dressed in buckskin from head to toe. I felt like I had stepped back in time, back to when this land was still wild and free, when men were rough and tough and women were scarce. We chatted briefly with them before pitching our tents and cooking dinner, utilizing the last throes of daylight.

After dinner, Dodger and I walked back to talk to our new friends. We sat huddled by the warmth of the fire, drinking coffee from their old metal cups, and discussing several aspects of life in the early 1800's. Our foray into history covered trapping, local forts and trading beads. We learned that of all the trading bead colors, blue was the most important. They were so valuable because the Indians could not make blue beads. They were rare and you could often get an entire beaver hide for one blue bead. Doug then gave Dodger and me each a blue bead.

The conversation turned to the fine art of fire making and the many ways of building a fire. Knowing I would be on the trail for some time, Mike and Doug set me up with my own flint and steel pouch, complete with everything I would need to start a fire the primitive way. I enjoyed the evening tremendously, soaking up as much information as I could.

The next morning I stopped to tell Mike and Doug goodbye as I left camp. They were pouring their first cup of morning coffee as I entered their camp and asked them to pose for a picture in the early morning light. They would have a full day of preparation for the nearly thousand buckskin clad mountain men who would fill the park in the next few days.

We hiked nonstop until almost noon, when we decided to stop for a lunch break. We sat alone on the desolate backcountry road. Only a few cars had passed by us all morning, and we were surprised when a car came by and stopped. Again a plain clothed Deputy Sheriff stepped out and walked over to us. It seems we had been called in again.

He spoke, "Folks around here have been a bit uneasy with the convicts loose. They were caught this morning and it should calm down after the news gets out. I came out to check things out to ease their minds. Y'all have a good day."

We hiked through a nicely wooded section of Oklahoma, and the afternoon hike was filled with visits from many species of birds. We saw Scissor-tailed Flycatchers, Coopers Hawks, Sparrows, Woodpeckers, Blue Jays, Blue Birds, Starlings, and a host of other birds. I may have seen my first Eagle as well but did not get close enough to be sure.

A few days later we found ourselves on the outskirts of Ardmore, where the Osage Indian Reservation was once located. Here Maria and Marjoria Tallchief were born. Along with Yvonne Chouteau, a Cherokee, Moscelyne Larkin of Peorian Indian descent, and Rosella Hightower, a Chickasaw Indian, they became the best Prima Ballerinas in the world during the late 1930's and early 1940's. No nation had ever been home to five women to aspire to this level at the same time before.

Maria Tallchief was considered the greatest ballerina of her day. She was born in 1925 and made her debut at the Hollywood Bowl when she was only fifteen. She became the highest paid ballerina ever, and received a Kennedy Center Gold Medal for lifetime contribution to the performing arts, America's highest honor for a performing artist.

There is so much to learn in Oklahoma—from mountain men one day to prima ballerinas the next.

Finally we made it to Dodgers house, covering some seventy-seven taxing miles in four days. Four days of hiking with pain involved on each and every step. My left foot was swollen and it hurt to stand, let alone walk. I hobbled to the kitchen, where Mrs. Ham had breakfast cooking and a good cup of coffee waiting for me. Chatting with Dodger, we decided the right thing to do was to take yet another day off. I was frustrated. I came here to hike, to see the country, but I can't very well do that without two good feet.

Instead of sitting in the house all day, Dodger suggested we go see some of Oklahoma that we had not planned to walk through. We drove to the 2,464-foot summit of Mt Scott, in the heart of the Wichita Mountains. To the east I could see the brown rolling hills of south-central Oklahoma. To the northwest lay the rest of the rough, jagged Wichita Mountains. The cold windy weather continued, and our stay on the summit was brief.

Our next stop led us to Fort Sill to see the grave of Geronimo. We were unable to find the Apache cemetery located on the still active fort, but did find the post cemetery. Quannah Parker was buried there, as well as more Native American Chiefs than in any other cemetery in the United States. It was a solemn place; tombstones lined white row after white row. Several government buildings surround the cemetery and a fence surrounds the perimeter of the fort, I had the feeling that the chiefs are still captive, even in death.

The day of rest had been a blessing, I felt much better and ready to start yet again. It was goodbye again for Dodger and his parents, and after another great home cooked breakfast we left Healdton behind as we had so many other little towns. We headed west across the dirt back roads that criss-cross the entire state. We left the wooded rolling hills, the land was flatter and trees quite sparse. Indeed, we were in the plains of western Oklahoma. The open fields provide an excellent winter habitat for the birds, however, and we were again blessed with an array of bird sightings: red tail hawks, ring tail hawks, kestrel hawks, starlings, meadowlarks, finches, pigeons, mockingbirds, several kinds of woodpeckers, sparrows, thrushes, chickadees, crows, cardinals, ducks, robins ... and the list goes on.

The next morning Dodger and I headed out with a beautiful blue sky above and a cool northeasterly wind blowing at our backs. We could see a monument ahead, on the crest of a rolling hill. When we reached it, we discovered that we were standing in the tracks of the historic Chisholm Trail. The high hill was a landmark along the trail. It was used by thousands of cowboys as they herded millions of cattle north to the Union Pacific

Railroad shipping yard in Abilene, Kansas. I felt a sense of pride as I stood on the bluff looking out at the vast plains.

I sat and let my imagination ramble freely; winding back some one hundred and sixty years ago as the cattle drive was on. I dreamt of sitting around the chuck wagon, as the cattle muddled around the area, the sun sitting low, and the smell of manure permeating the air. I smiled to think of how rugged those men were, how free they were.

We reached Waurika Lake at about 4:30 and set up camp before cooking dinner. I was filled with joy, grateful to be enjoying my life of freedom, hiking from place to place, making new friends, and enjoying the spacious beauty that is Oklahoma.

As the sun fell into the western sky, the coyotes once again began to howl. They were very close, and their song was vibrant and clear. Soon the sun disappeared and the night air turned crisp. Slowly, the sky painted itself one dot at a time, creating the masterpiece that we are blessed to see every night. Dodger and I sat up and talked as late as we could, finally being driven into the warmth of our tents by the cold night air.

In the middle of the night I woke up and crawled out of my tent. The world stood still; there was not a sound, just a perfect sky with the haze of the Milky Way Galaxy high above me and millions of stars beyond that. The sky was absolutely entrancing. To the south I could see Wichita Falls, Texas, lighting up the horizon. To the north and east were thousands of lights across the horizon from small towns across miles and miles of Oklahoma. I gazed in awe until I could no longer stand the cold and again had to crawl back into the warmth of my sleeping bag. It was an incredible moment of peace and harmony; a moment when you know you belong here.

The next morning I woke to find my tent frosted over, inside and out. I had not left enough of my windows open, and my breath condensed on the inside walls, then froze. I was toasty warm in my sleeping bag, but my tent was icy. All was fine until the sun warmed the day, and my tent began to melt—and drip. I was up and moving earlier than I had planned, as Dodger laughed at my misfortune.

When I crossed into eastern Oklahoma last December, I was still very much in the southeast. I now however was undoubtedly in the west. I encountered my first tumbleweed followed quickly by my second, third, and five-hundredth. They appeared and were everywhere at times. They came blowing across the field, or down the road. I quickly became very good at dodging them.

I also passed a flock of geese, several thousand strong. They were nestled in a large pasture. Wanting to get a good close-up picture, I did my best Wild Kingdom impersonation as Dodger watched, laughing all the while. Have you ever seen two to three thousand geese take off at the same time? They flew up into the sky, made a big circle and nestled back down, deeper into the field and farther from me. There would be no pictures. Later in the day, however, we passed two more flocks flying north—a sure sign of the approaching spring.

The road hike ran for twelve miles before turning north to rejoin with Route 70. We walked the entire twelve miles without seeing a single car. This Route 70 is the same Route 70 that I hiked on in Tennessee near my aunt's house. It is the same Route 70 that is part of the Appalachian Trail, Main Street in Hot Springs, North Carolina.

We reached our last town in Oklahoma, the town of Davidson, around 3:00 and bought supplies for the night. It was only two more miles to the Red River, our campsite for the night. About halfway between town and the river we passed Lambs Tavern and could hear live country music coming from inside. We could not pass it up and stopped to see the band. Inside we dusted off our throats as we talked with Mr. Lamb and his wife, the owners of the little pub.

We were soon back on the road, and reached the shore of the Red River at 5:00. We had company, as Saturdays are busy days in the sandy bowels of the river. There were at least twenty four-wheelers riding around in the sand, the constant noise of the high-pitched engines resonating throughout the valley.

Dodger and I talked with several of them asking where the best campsites would be for us, so we could keep out of their way, and enjoy the river. They were having a cookout and invited us to join in their feast of hot sausage sandwiches and grilled pork chops. We were more than happy to join them and enjoyed dinner with them. We learned that most of them called Vernon, Texas home, which is where we would be staying the next night.

As the sun began to sink and the air cooled, most of them headed for home. Dodger and I hiked back to our tents on the riverbank to watch the show the sunset promised to give. We were not disappointed. The clouds in the western sky lit up as did the entire western horizon, a bright glow of burning, fading fire.

Camping on the banks of the Red River. I could see Texas. It was just on the other side. Oklahoma had been a treasure, and I felt blessed to have seen as much of it as I have. Three young men stayed to watch the sunset with us, and chat. We talked for some time about the trek in great detail, as well as stars scouting, and life. We were all looking up when a shooting star came across the northern sky. I laid in my tent, three feet from the Red River, the river so famous in western history.

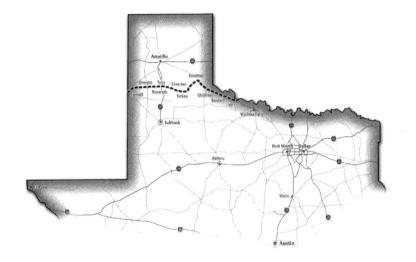

Texas

I awoke in time to watch the sun peak over the eastern horizon. Next to me, the Red River flowed effortlessly eastward, the giant ball of fire seemingly drawing the river to itself until they collided on the horizon.

We packed our gear taking care to leave the sand in the river bottom and out of our packs. As we walked towards the bridge, Dodger was hobbling badly. He had twisted his foot the day before, but had no real problem then. This morning however, it was a different story; he was now in severe pain.

We stopped at the "Welcome to Texas" sign for a picture, but my excitement was overshadowed by the possibility that I could lose Dodger again soon. We climbed out of the valley, leaving the river behind us and discovered the wind, which was blowing very hard right at us. Each step was a chore and I felt like I was hiking with ankle weights on. After a mile or so Dodger's foot loosened up; he was hiking better. He was afraid to stop however, knowing that his foot would again stiffen and he would have to suffer the pain of starting out again. We put our heads down and hiked the fifteen miles to Vernon without a break. Once in town we found a hotel and a chance to rest.

The next morning I talked Dodger into walking uptown with me to see if new shoes might help. As we walked and talked, Dodger limped along until he finally confided to me that his foot hurt deeply and he didn't think that new shoes were the answer. He wanted to see a doctor.

We turned around and hobbled back to the hotel and he called home. His parents would come and get him.

"I'll take today off and wait for your parents with you," I offered.

"You need to make miles; they will be here in a few hours. Besides, I don't like long goodbyes. I am sorry," Dodger quietly replied.

I slowly packed my gear, not knowing what else to do but to keep on hiking. We hugged goodbye, both of us pained with his need to return home. With my heart heavy at the misfortune of my friend, and my backpack full of dreams, I walked out alone to see Texas. By nightfall Dodger was back in the comfort of his house physically, but mentally he was somewhere in Texas with me. Somewhere in Texas, that's where I would spend the night.

The sky above was a never-ending blue, and the wind on the ground was just as never-ending—blowing unabated across the barren plains. I had no clear destination in mind. I had gotten out of town much too late to make it the twenty-nine miles to Quannah, the next sizable town.

I hiked all afternoon into the wind, which had maintained a steady fifteen to twenty miles per hour gust. I trudged along, fighting it every step of the way, eventually reaching the small town of Chillicothe, home of a Dairy Queen and a gas station. The wind was not as fierce in town, and I contemplated staying. My map showed a creek about three miles west of town, so I decided to finish dinner and then hike on.

I figured there would be some trees near the creek, and they would provide a windbreak and a place to camp. I never found it. I pushed on, worn out from the steady uphill hike into the wind. I pushed on, seeing nothing but endless open fields with nothing to break the wind and thunderheads forming on the horizon. I pushed on, in search of somewhere in Texas.

I was in the high plains and quickly learning that it can be very unforgiving. The wind was blowing so hard I had concerns about setting my tent up with no protection from the wind. I considered crawling under the highway into the cattle runs. The square four-foot high concrete structures sure looked inviting. They were clean and certainly high enough to sit up in, but if rained, they would flood and I would be in big trouble. I decided this was a foolish idea and kept walking along, hoping to find somewhere to get out of the oppressive wind.

I finally found two old train boxcars sitting in a field. Other than the cattle that called this desolate wind-tortured place home, there was nothing else in sight—just two rusted, brown, out-of-place boxcars. I jumped the fence and scurried across the field, jumping into the first car. Inside, it was calm and had a clean wooden floor. The open window allowed plenty of light to get in. Yes, this would make a fine home for the night.

I stood peering through my boxcar window, watching the sun set behind the storm that was moving across the plains. I could see the rain falling to the southwest. Fortunately, it stayed south, and I stayed dry. As it turned darker and colder, I crawled into my sleeping bag, bedding down like an old hobo. I lay there thinking how glad I was to have a warm dry place to get out of the weather, and wondering if Dodger had made it home.

I slept well in my private car, waking around 7:30 feeling very good. I packed and hit the road, and after a few miles the landscape changed. The land was spotted with dense areas of scrub oak. I hoped this would continue, as it would provide a place to camp when needed.

I reached the town of Quannah in time for lunch.
The town was named in honor of Quannah Parker, one of
the last pre-reservation Comanche Chiefs. He was a fierce
warrior who resisted reservation life as long as he could.
His father was also a Comanche Chief and was killed in
battle while he was still a young man. His mother was a
white woman who had been captured at the age of nine and
raised as a Comanche. A short time after his father was
killed, his mother was recaptured by the whites and
returned to her white family. She had spent most of her life
as a Comanche and did not fit in with the white society.
She longed to return to the tribe, but died a few years later,
never seeing any of her three children again. They say she
died of a broken heart. Quanah took his mother's white last
name to honor her.

After the Red River War of 1874 – 1875, Quannah
ended up on the reservation and did his best to represent his
people. He visited Washington, D.C. several times, and
was a friend of Theodore Roosevelt. He was proud of the
town named after him and visited it often before he passed
away in 1911. He was buried at Fort Sill, Oklahoma, near
his mother and sister.

I spent the next few days hiking from ghost town to
ghost town, following along the very busy Texas Highway
287. Later that afternoon I reached the town of Acme. In
1890 a fellow named James Sickler discovered gypsum
there. He gathered some partners and the Lone Star
Cement Plaster Company and the town of Acme was born.
The town had a hotel, railroad depot, general store and a
school. Like many towns of the day, the company owned
most of the houses and their employees paid rent back to
them. The factory still stands, and is now run by Georgia
Pacific. The town, however, has long since disappeared

and just a few scattered ruins remain. The 1990 census reports that fourteen people still live in Acme, though I saw no sign of that.

I reached the small town of Goodlett before sunset. When cotton was king, this was a booming town as well, but again not much is left. The old cotton gin still stands and is now a museum at the Old Cotton Gin RV Park. Norma, the owner invited me in. She had seen me walking earlier and had expected to see me tonight. She refused to let me pay for a spot to pitch my tent and even gave me a phone to plug into the outlet at the campsite. We talked for some time before I walked out and pitched my tent in the yard, watching the sun slip out of sight to give way to the stars on another beautiful Texas night. I called Dodger and learned he fractured his foot and would not be returning. I would be alone all the way to California.

The next morning, I was up with the sun and gone with the wind—gone into the wind was more like it. The headwind blew steadily at twenty-five or thirty mph all day, and when the trucks came rolling past me, it was even worse. I walked along, lunging head long, into the gale. The force of the truck-enhanced wind stopped me dead in my tracks, and I was left with my foot suspended in mid air for a second as each truck rushed by me. Fortunately, I found refuge for lunch in the next ghost town, Kirkland, Texas. Like so many other towns in the panhandle, there is nothing left, just a few deserted houses and some old cotton equipment.

Late that afternoon a Texas State Trooper stopped me. He was very polite as he asked for my ID and then walked back to his car to run a background check on me. He must have thought I was a vagrant, and seemed surprised to find my driver's license valid and clean. He asked me what I was doing out there. I told him I had come to see America, and meet her people. He just shook his head when I told him I owned a car that I left sitting in Ohio. I had cleared waivers again, and he wished me well as I hiked on.

The next morning I finally left the busy highway and headed out across a quiet back road. I had been watching a mesa in the distance all day, and I was finally hiking towards it. Sometime in the day, I would walk past that flat-topped mound of earth rising up from the plains. I crossed the rolling hills, gazing out across the ravines and endless prairie all around me.

I felt sluggish most of the day and finally realized I was probably dehydrated. I needed to drink more water. Four different times I had cars stop along the quiet back road to make sure I was OK, and to offer me a ride. I thanked each of them, then watched them speed off, continuing on at my own steady pace.

I reached the mesa late in the afternoon, and ended up camping near it, alone on the prairie. After I settled into to camp, I discovered I only thought I was alone. I had several jack rabbits for company and they scuttled around my tent long after I had gone to sleep.

The next day I reached the small town of Turkey, Texas, birthplace of country singer Bob Wills. My first stop was at the convenience store for some Gatorade and a snack. I then hiked right down Main Street in search of the Turkey Hotel. I heard the long closed hotel had been reopened. When I arrived, I met Matt and his sister Michelle. They were spending the night also, and were heading out in the morning to hike the Caprock Canyon Trail. I met hikers! I had not seen another hiker since Dodger and I were in Kentucky.

Little did I know the trail existed, and I could have hiked it for the previous twenty miles. Matt and Michelle would be headed to the southern end of it to hike in the morning, but I would be able to hike out of Turkey on it for a while, as I continued southwest.

The beautiful old hotel was built in 1927. It has been restored and is now operating as a bed & breakfast. The hotel is truly from a different era, when plumbing was very expensive and communal bathrooms were normal. This was an upscale place however, and had a bathroom between every two rooms, instead of one per floor.

The hotel was built with hopes of helping the young town grow, but as better methods were developed for shipping cotton, the railroad lost its importance, and the town its promise of growth. This is farm country, and the towns that have survived are wonderful little places, full of charm and good people.

Dinner was about to be served, and Matt asked if there would be enough for me. The three of us sat at the dinner table eating and talking until 8:30 that evening. I was in need of a bath and so we took a short break before meeting again in the lobby to talk some more. It was so good to see hikers.

The next morning I was in no hurry as I hadn't planned on a long day. I sat and enjoyed coffee with the owner and staff before heading out along the Caprock Canyon Trail. It felt good to be off the pavement for a while.

Along the trail was a historical marker telling of the J.A. Ranch. John Adair originally owned it, and Charles Goodnight managed it. In 1883, the ranch was situated on 1.3 million acres and had 100,000 Hereford cattle.

Hereford remained the mainstay of the cattle population
until 1998; today the ranch is predominantly Black Angus
and Charolais. While the name of the cattle stock has
changed, the ranch remains in the hands of the Adair family
to this day. When Mrs. Adair died in 1921 in England, her
grandson Montie Ritchie showed an interest in their
American property. He fully assumed the management in
1935 and worked the ranch until 1991 when he retired.
Today his daughter Ninia runs the ranch.

    I reached the town of Quiteque at about 1:30, the
end of the trail section for me. I ate lunch in town and then
called Nina. She hoped to come visit me in New Mexico,
and planned to join me in California so we could hike the
Pacific Crest Trail together. I headed west with a bounce in
my step, despite being loaded with enough water to get me
the seventeen miles to Silverton.

    Before me lay the Caprock Rim, looming five
hundred feet above the valley floor where I stood, certainly,
the largest climb I had seen in hundreds of miles. The area
was breathtaking with deep rugged, barren ravines running
throughout and small pines dotting the fields. I climbed
steadily, and once on top reached a picnic overlook. I
stopped for a break to celebrate reaching the two thousand
mile mark for the trek. I was excited to be in the mountains
again, and considered spending the night. The weather
forecast called for a cold front to move in the next
afternoon, so I had to move on.

    Around 4:30, I was again hiking, hoping to hike just
three more miles back down the other side of the mountain
I had just climbed. There was no other side. The five
hundred-foot climb was simply a climb to higher plains.
Once on top I did not go back down, but indeed continued

to climb ever so gradually. I stood at 3,800 feet and was out of the mountains. All my nice campsites were gone.

The road sign read: "Silverton 10." It was 5:15 now, it would be after eight and dark by the time I got that far. My map showed a municipal airport, and I was sure they would have a hotel. I was concerned about the weather report for the next afternoon and decided it was important to make as many miles as possible today. It was not long before the sun set and the night air turned colder. I donned my fleece top and gloves, but remained in my short pants. I was cold by the time I reached town at 8:15. I stopped at the convenience store, got some dinner, and inquire about a hotel. No hotel in town was the answer.

I walked back outside and looked around town. I saw a church steeple not far away. I walked back inside to introduce myself to the store clerk and inform her I would be camped in the churchyard. When I arrived at the church a car pulled in and a man got out. He was headed inside when I approached him to ask permission to camp. He was an elder, and saw no problem with me tenting for the night.

I set up camp and had just gotten into my sleeping bag, nice and warm, when headlights pulled right up the edge of my tent. It was the deputy sheriff. He wanted to see some identification, and "check me out." Just like the last officer, he was courteous. He called the church pastor to inform him of my presence. The pastor offered to let me sleep inside, as it was supposed to get cold. I declined because my tent was already up and I was comfortable.

The twenty-seven mile day had a price as my right foot had developed a nasty blister. I hoped a good night's rest would help it; it had to, as I was still twenty-eight miles from the next town and refuge from the severe wind and cold forecast for tomorrow.

I was up at first light and hiking. I would have to push hard to make it to town. I climbed steadily, above four thousand feet. I passed the first named stream since I crossed over the Red River one hundred forty miles ago ... it was dry.

Shortly thereafter, I reached the site of one of the battles that occurred during the Red River War. General Mackenzie's soldiers destroyed the village of Red Warbonnet. Most of the Indians abandoned everything, even their horses, as they fled the canyon for the open plains. In the aftermath, Mackenzie's troops captured over 1,400 ponies. About 350 were given away and the rest were shot. The Indians' entire winter food supply was also destroyed. The battle at Palo Duro Canyon was the Plains Indians' last major battle against the land hungry white settlers.

At 1:30, the temperature was still fifty degrees and I hiked along in my short-sleeve shirt. By 2:00, it was getting windy. By 3:00, the temperature was below freezing and the wind was howling at thirty to forty miles an hour. My radio reported that the wind-chill was only eight degrees.

The open plains offered no refuge and the wind howled down on me from the north, crashing into my right side. I leaned into it and used my hiking poles to help keep my balance. I trudged on, still eleven miles from the safety of the town. I had not expected it to get so cold so quickly.

Despite having on every piece of clothing I owned, I was cold and getting colder. Somewhere in the wind I lost my green bandana. It had been with me since I started the Appalachian Trail in March 1999, and had traveled over 4,200 miles with me.

I hiked on in pain; my feet hurt, as the blister had gotten no better. My hands were freezing cold, and my cheeks were numb. I could see the water tower in town, still five miles away, it seemed to be always out there, but never getting closer. About two miles from town, a truck pulled beside me. The window came down and the gentleman inside asked if I needed a ride. I had only a moment to decide. I was so cold and determined the intelligent thing to do was to get out of the arctic wind tunnel and seek refuge. Heroes die. It was the first and only ride I accepted on the walk.

The weather the next morning was no better as the wind continued to howl and the temperature remained bitterly cold. My mood matched that of the weather; I had a serious case of loneliness. I spent the morning writing to friends. Tonight was forecast to again be bitterly cold, so I decided to hike the thirty miles to Dimmitt in two days. I would hike part of the way one day and return to the hotel for the night. I would then hitch a ride to the county line, where I stopped the first day, and resume hiking. I had no clue how I would get back, but had faith I would.

The wind had calmed down and shortly after lunch I headed out of the hotel and crossed Interstate 27. A mile down the road I reached a Texas State Prison. This brought serious concern to me, as I realized how hard it could be to hitch hike near a prison. I walked on past, that would be a problem to deal with tomorrow. Today I was glad to be able to make a few miles, and walked steadily on until I reached the county line. I stopped and turned around, sticking my thumb out to get a ride back to where I had just started. In short time a car stopped and I was back at the hotel.

I enjoyed breakfast at the hotel restaurant before once again heading west towards Dimmitt. I crossed the interstate and could see the prison just ahead. I thought that there was no way I was going to get a ride standing next to this prison.

Two minutes later an eastbound car pulled up and the driver said, "Are you Dan?"

I was taken by surprise; I had never seen this man before. I quickly replied, "Yes, I am."

The car pulled over and the man again spoke "get in--it's freezing out there!" He smiled and added, "My name is Earl. Earl Needham. I live in Clovis, New Mexico and have been following your journey from your online journal. I figured you would be getting close, so I came to check on you!"

He brought water, lemonade, cookies, and a ride to the county line. What incredible trail magic. We talked, and in no time reached the county line. We stopped and talked awhile longer. Before he left, he gave me his phone number should I need anything the next week or so. His kindness, completely unexpected, pure and unconditional, lifted me out of the funk I'd been in the past few days.

I watched his car speed out of sight as I continued under the blue skies. The temperature climbed to the mid-forties, and the wind was not so cold. Strong is another thing. It was a steady twenty-five or thirty miles an hour with gusts up to forty. I often had to lean into it. I was again all bundled up to protect myself. I had hiked about six miles when I reached the small town of Nazareth, population about four hundred.

I stopped in at the 19th Hole Café to get out of the wind for a bit. I ordered a cup of coffee and a piece of cake. There were ten locals there, and the place had an upbeat, friendly atmosphere. As I paid, the cashier told me a young lady at the table behind me had bought my coffee. I thanked her and then walked out to my pack. As I put my pack on it occurred to me that I should go back in. I grabbed some of my business cards and announced to the crowd why I was out there. I told several stories of my journey and finally thanked them for the friendship. I left with well wishes from everyone.

As I left town, I noticed a placard proclaiming the prowess of the town's high-school women's basketball team—fifteen state titles in the past twenty-five years. That is an incredible run for any team. Incredible. I also noticed the wind had stopped. As quickly as it had come, it had disappeared. I started shedding clothes and wondering where the wind goes when it leaves.

I was cruising along when I noticed my shoes were literally falling apart. I stopped and wrapped them with duct tape. I would be in Clovis New Mexico soon, and hoped they would make it that far. I reached Dimmitt in great spirits; elated with the people and experiences I had encountered.

The next morning put me right back into the wide-open prairie. The cold front had passed on and it was a magnificent day for hiking, and soaring, or so the Geese thought. I passed several flocks, each containing thousands of birds. They swarmed above me flying in circles, seemingly unsure if it was time to go north just yet or not.

Ahead on the horizon I saw a clump of trees, a sure sign that a house was ahead. They were planted to break the wind and protect the house. It is rare to find trees without a house, and out here rarely do you find more than one or two houses together.

I hiked through the small near-ghost town of Hub late in the day. The town was merely a collection of houses with several of them abandoned. There were no stores or businesses, just a dozen or so houses. I walked to the west edge of town, to the last abandoned house. I pitched my tent in the yard and began to cook dinner. No sooner had I finished eating when I got company. Two local dogs had smelled me and came to investigate. They were very friendly and I made the critical mistake of petting them— friends for life. They were disappointed when I crawled into my tent, but being the friends that we were, they stayed with me all night, sleeping just outside the tent. Every now and then, they would peek through the mesh windows to see if I was still there.

The morning was again bitter cold as another front moved in. I bid my canine friends farewell, bundled up and headed for New Mexico. My friend Earl stopped by again shortly after ten. He brought me a sausage biscuit for breakfast. He was surprised to see me so far along, nearly in the town of Bovina. We sat in his car and chatted for thirty minutes before I resumed hiking.

The afternoon wind picked up considerably and the temperature again dropped. I reached the New Mexico state line, leaving Texas in my rear view mirror. The bustling border town of Texico was a welcome sight as my shoes were worn out. I planned to pick up a pair of boots that my mother had mailed to me. I went to the first hotel I saw, the Crossroads Hotel.

I inquired to the seventy-eight year old woman running the cozy little place "Have you got a room for an old hiker?"

"Where ya hiking from?" she asked.

I told her of my grand adventure, but she was not impressed.

"I think you're stupid for hiking around. You should be working. There is so much work to do, and good help is so hard to find. You should have a job. Yes I have a room, it will be $40 and I only take cash!"

I was low on cash, so I ran across the street to the convenience store and the ATM machine. I reappeared, undaunted by her dislike of my adventure, and smiled, offering her the $40.

"I am sorry I was so rude to you," she opened. "I have just had a very bad day. I really don't treat my customers this way." We talked for another half-hour as I learned of her troubles, and she learned more of my adventure.

"That'll be $35 for the room," she finally said with a smile of her own. I had made a friend.

Outside, the wind was gusting up to fifty mph. The temperature was in the low twenties and would drop to twelve that night. The wind chill would be well below zero and I was grateful to be safely tucked away.

I sat in my room and reflected back on Texas; I thought of the physical and mental trials it had bestowed upon me. It still could not believe I had lost Dodger again. My face and hands were both sunburned and wind burned. I had been chilled to the core several times by the unforgiving winds.

Texas had also been full of rewards, as I had been blessed with meeting so many good souls, and enjoyed seeing the high plains that I had only ever known from John Wayne movies.

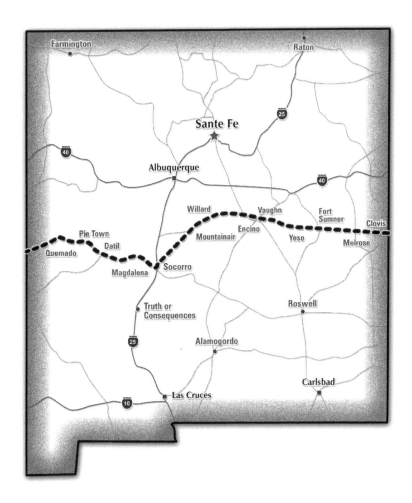

New Mexico

I holed up for a day in Texico, waiting for the weather to break. The following day the wind calmed and I took the opportunity to continue west. The twelve-mile hike to Clovis was a test run for the new boots my mother had mailed me. It went fairly well, though my feet were tender by the end of the day. I reached the east end of Clovis by early afternoon. and stopped at McDonald's for a cup of hot coffee to warm me. When you walk into a place with a backpack on, you really stick out. People generally stare at you because they are curious. As usual, I struck up a conversation with some of them, breaking down the walls of mystery that had surrounded me when I walked in. With my coffee gone, it was time to resume hiking into the center of town to find a hotel and refuge from the bitter cold that would return with nightfall.

Clovis is home of the world famous Norman Petty recording studio. In February of 1957, Buddy Holly and his band, the Crickets, recorded their version of "That'll be the Day" here, launching him into superstardom. Roy Orbison and Waylon Jennings also recorded here. The last star to record at the studio was LeAnn Rimes, who recorded her #1 hit "Blue" here in 1996.

Clovis is also a main hub on the Santa Fe rail system; the main line from Chicago to Bakersfield runs through here. The town was built because the Santa Fe Rail Company wanted a terminal in eastern New Mexico, so they built it in the middle of the prairie and the town grew around it. A rail official's daughter named the town. Clovis was the first Christian king of the Frankish Empire, and she liked the name.

That night I enjoyed dinner with my friend Earl that I had met near Dimmitt Texas. Earl is retired from the Air Force, and is a large, soft-spoken man who loves to tinker. His car, equipped with a short wave radio and a GPS system, is ready for anything. He gave me some good advice about walking across the barren high desert plains that lay ahead.

I didn't sleep well and felt sluggish the next morning but was out of the hotel and hiking by nine. As soon as I left the sidewalks of Clovis, I saw the Air Force jets of Cannon Air Force Base, which lies just a few miles west. I was hiking in my short pants for the first time in several days, the warmth of the sunshine a welcome friend.

Once beyond the Air Force Base, I got a taste of how desolate Route 60 is. Traffic practically disappeared. The grassy brown landscape looked inhospitable and I watched several tumbleweed tornadoes as they blew across the open rolling hills. I was about twelve miles into the day's journey when my feet began to hurt, especially my left heel.

I kept moving on, but the pain in my feet became more intense. I hiked another three miles and could go no farther. I stopped and took my boots off. My feet were red and swollen from heel to toe, and both heels were badly blistered. I had never blistered like this before. I took my safety pin out and plunged it into the half-dollar sized blisters on each heel, draining them and relieving the pressure, and hopefully the pain.

If I could make it three more miles, I would be in St Vrain, the next dot on my map. I knew there was a post office there; perhaps I could use their phone to call Earl. I was sure that my new boots were the reason my feet were so blistered. I desperately needed to get back to Clovis for a different pair of shoes, as there would not be another town large enough to have a shoe store in the next two hundred miles.

I hobbled on for another ninety minutes, using my hiking poles as crutches. I finally reached the congested area that calls itself St. Vrain. As I passed the first of the five or six houses in town, I saw a phone booth near a small roadside picnic area—little victories. It was my hope that Earl would be home and would be able to help me get another pair of shoes. I reached the phone booth only to find an empty case; the phone had been removed. I still had hope of using the phone at the post office. I hobbled another hundred yards or so to the post office. The door was locked; it closes at 12:30 PM daily.

My feeling of reprieve was quickly replaced with deep concern. I sat down on the steps, staring out at the desert that was now my home and again drained my blisters and aired out my poor, battered feet. I was in serious pain, but again all I could do was press on. It was still seven more miles to the larger town of Melrose, where I had planned to spend the night.

As I left St. Vrain, my stride was reduced to baby steps. Every step brought intense pain, as if twenty needles were being pushed deeply into my left heel. I changed my step so that I never stepped onto my left heel, walking on my toes. I hobbled along, and after an hour I could see the water tower on the horizon, still five miles away. I kept moving, slow and steady, trying to get my mind onto something else. It was useless; my mind was polluted with pain.

After nearly four hours and the seven hardest, most painful miles I had ever walked, I reached Melrose and a phone. I called Earl but got no answer. I sat outside the store in the dark of early evening, the night chill beginning to set in. I had no idea where to camp, and was certainly not up to exploring the town and its surrounding area to find a spot. I had to find a way back to Clovis to get new shoes, and to rest my tattered appendages called feet.

I walked inside and asked to see a phone book. I then called a cab company back in Clovis to come and get me. It would take them an hour to make the twenty-two miles journey from Clovis. I sat and waited, glad to be off my feet. I would deal with everything else in the morning.

I drained my blisters and hobbled down to the restaurant for breakfast. I had gotten in touch with Earl overnight and he came by to join me. We went to the mall where I bought a pair of New Balance shoes, similar to the ones I wore across Oklahoma and Texas. The rest of the day was spent in Earl's little car, exploring the vast area south of Clovis.

The next morning my feet felt much better and I decided I could continue. Earl came by and took me back to Melrose. He offered to come and check on me later, to make sure I was OK. I would have to make good miles, as it was thirty-seven miles to my next water source. I planned to be in Fort Sumner in just two days.

I had put in about six and a half miles when Earl returned. He pulled off just ahead of me at a historical marker. It was a memorial to the millions of bison that once roamed freely across the western plains and to the Native Americans who once lived there. Earl and I talked for twenty minutes before he had to head back home. He is truly a trail angel if I have ever seen one. We bid a final farewell and as I walked on, I knew I had been blessed to meet him.

I could not help but daydream of what an incredible sight it must have been to see the endless fields in front of me covered with bison. Standing six feet high and weighing more than two thousand pounds, they are the largest North American mammals. Before Europeans set foot in the west, there were more than thirty million bison roaming between the Mississippi River and the Rocky Mountains. Their seemingly inexhaustible numbers did little to protect them from the unbelievable onslaught that came with western expansion. As part of the war waged against the Plains Indians, the creatures were slaughtered by the millions and left in heaping piles to rot in the oppressive summer sun. By the end of the nineteenth century there were only five hundred left. Today, due to an solid preservation effort, there are nearly fifty thousand again, roaming the west on refuges and ranches.

I spent the day watching as train after train passed by me, some going east, some going west, all loaded with commercial goods on their way to market. I watched them approach me from miles away, and listened to the howling of their whistles as they rolled past. Next to the tracks was a dirt service road. I decided to hike on it, as it would be much easier on my feet.

I was glad to be in New Mexico, excited to be out in the open plains, out where you can see from horizon to horizon, and the sky seems to go on forever. I had just stopped to refill my drinking bottle from a supply bottle in my pack when a car pulled over. Out of the car jumped Mike and Jeff Smith, two fellow hikers I had met in Virginia the year before. They too had been following my journey on the Internet and had driven down from

Albuquerque to find me. We hugged, laughed, and talked for nearly an hour before they had to get back home. I hiked a few more miles before finding a campsite. As I sat cooking dinner, two black crows visited me. They flew so close that I could hear their wings flapping in the wind. I was alone in the quiet of dusk, happy with my new shoes and the health of my feet, happy to be exploring New Mexico.

The next day brought a change of scenery as the Taiban Mesa lay to the north of me, and a mountain rising several thousand feet into the air dominated the distant southern landscape. I passed several isolated houses scattered about the area. At least half of them were deserted, the solitude and difficulty in growing anything here seemingly too much for some of the former inhabitants to bear. It was a lonely place.

I reached the major town of Fort Sumner in mid-afternoon, the largest town for sixty miles east and one hundred twenty miles west. There are about 1,200 people living in the town, more than half of the total population for the county. About three miles south of town lies the grave of Billy the Kid. I wanted to see the gravesite, but since it was a six-mile round trip, I decided to not walk down and back. I did stop at the Billy the Kid Museum in town to learn more about the boy outlaw, however.

He was born William Henry Bonney in 1860 or 1861, no one knows for sure when, or where. His tombstone lists his birth date as November 23, 1860. The first record of him can be traced to Anderson, Indiana, in 1868. He never knew his father. Shortly after he was born, his mother, Catherine, married a fellow named McCarty and Billy's name became William McCarty. In 1873 Catherine married again, this time to William Antrim, and the new family moved to Silver City, New Mexico. She died the following year and Billy and his younger brother were left on the streets by their stepfather, who wanted nothing to do with them.

Billy worked odd jobs to support himself, and eventually got on as a ranch hand. He was a fine-looking young man and got along well with the ladies, but the older ranch hands often picked on him. During a scuffle one day, he killed a man in self-defense. Frightened, he fled the area and his legend began.

He fought in the Lincoln County War in 1878. The war was between two ranchers fighting over land rights. Billy killed several men during the war. The problem for Billy was that the side he chose to fight for lost, and the other side was full of the corrupt politicians who ruled New Mexico at the time. The governor had granted immunity to all those involved in the Lincoln County War, but Billy had murder charges filed against him anyhow. He escaped from the jail, as he had done every other time he was caught. He fled, running for his life, knowing he would never get a fair trial.

On July 14, 1881, Sheriff Pat Garret, who was hiding in the bedroom at Pete Maxwell's house, gunned down Billy, who was unarmed. After shooting him, the Sheriff and Pete ran outside to safety, fearing retaliation from the quick, accurate cowboy. There was no need to worry, however, as the shot had hit him in the heart and he quickly died. The next day he was buried next to his pals Tom O'Folliard and Charlie Bowdre. One of the most visited graves in the United States, it sits inside a cage to keep people from rubbing the stone smooth. I find it ironic that a man who escaped every cell he was ever put into is now buried behind bars.

Those who knew him spoke highly of him, commending his humorous and joyful manner. Hijinio Salazar said of Billy, "Billy the Kid was the bravest man I ever knew. He did not know what fear meant. Everyone who knew him loved him. He was kind and good to poor people, and he was always a gentleman, no matter where he was. He was quick as a kitten and when he aimed his pistol and fired, something dropped; he never missed his mark."

Pete Maxwell was the son of Lucien Maxwell, who at one time owned more land than any other American, 1.7 million acres. That is 2,680 square miles, more than twice the size of Rhode Island. His land was originally developed in 1862 as the original Fort Sumner. It was built to house 8,000 rebellious Navajo Indians who were causing trouble in the four corners region. The men, women and children of the Navajo nation were force-marched three hundred arduous miles across New Mexico to the area known as Bosque Renondo, now Fort Sumner. It was much different than the bountiful majestic mountains they had left behind. They remained imprisoned on the reservation until 1868, when a treaty was negotiated between General William T. Sherman and the Navajo Nation. President Andrew Johnson signed it into law and it allowed the Navajo to return to their native lands. Fort Sumner closed shortly there after. The treaty acknowledged the sovereignty of the Navajo and established the legal foundation for the modern Navajo Nation. With a population of over 175,000 on the Navajo Reservation, their people and culture is alive and well today.

Nina and I talked every time I made it to town. I missed her terribly, and she had decided to visit me for my birthday in another week. She would fly into Albuquerque,

some two hours north of where I would be hiking. We had
grown very close during my winter break, and I looked
forward to seeing her again.

I had also been in touch with Allan Stibora, who
lived in Mountainair. He had emailed me and planned to
meet me the next day to drop some water caches along the
road. This would help me get across the one hundred plus
miles of desolate plains ahead.

I was out early the next morning, headed west out
of town. I crossed the Pecos River, a small fast-flowing
river that is the lifeline of this community. It was the first
running stream I had seen since the Red River more than
330 miles before. I crossed the river and began to climb,
leaving Fort Sumner behind and finding myself alone on
the high plains. The town of Vaughn was sixty miles away.
Beyond that, it was another sixty-seven miles to
Mountainair, where I would meet Nina.

As I reached the top of the hill, the wind began to
blow. It was coming straight at me, and I trudged on
through it. It was fierce, blowing thirty or thirty-five miles
per hour, and at times gusting to near fifty. Along with the
wind came dust storms. I often had to turn my back to take
cover as a massive dust storm blew past me. Aluminum
cans and tumbleweeds blew by me. Fortunately, I was able
to dodge them and was not hit. It took all my strength to
cover three miles per hour.

The wind continued to beat me up, and after about
eight miles, my Pop-Tart breakfast had worn off; I was
starving. I saw an abandoned house ahead and decided to
get out of the wind for a break. There were no "No
Trespassing" signs, so I ducked in for lunch.

I finished lunch and headed back out into the
unrelenting wind. It was a physically demanding day, but

one filled with simple rewards. The endless brown, windy plains had something about them. A sense of simplicity, and complexity; of calm, and of fury, all at once. I saw wildlife often, and on this day I passed by a tiny field mouse doing his daily work, and five antelope. I reminded myself that I was walking through their home—that I was a visitor—and that long after I was gone, they would remain.

Eventually, I had to stop to fill my water bottle. I sat for a few minutes, airing out my tender feet and enjoying the day. A truck pulled up, and I knew it must be Allan. I walked to the road and got in. It felt good to be out of the wind again. As we sat and talked, he gave me a thermos of hot tea: how incredible! It felt very good on such a blustery day. He gave me a treasure map so I could locate my hidden water caches, and all too soon he was gone.

It had been a special week filled with friends: Earl, Mike, Jeff, and now Allan. I was grateful for them. I had spent several hundred miles alone, and even though I saw people when I passed through the small towns, I missed the camaraderie of friends, that common bond. The intense solitude was a challenge for me.

I reached the ghost town of Yeso late in the afternoon. It had once been a thriving little town, but that was a long, long time ago. The general store and gift shop still stood, but the buildings were roofless and rundown. The weathered brick walls were crumbling from decades of sitting silent. Three houses appeared to have people living in them, though, and amazingly enough there was a post office.

About a mile out of town, I reached my first water cache, located in a low spot that protected it from the still howling wind. I was able to pour the water from the Ziploc bag into my water container without spilling any. I had waited all day for the wind to soften, but it seemed to get harder the later it got. I was very tired, and I found home for the night in a tunnel under the road. It was a cattle tunnel used to move cattle from a field on one side of the road to the other. It had a ceiling six feet high with a clean, level dirt floor. More important, the wind was non-existent inside.

I enjoyed a cheese tortilla and watched the sun set before crawling into my sleeping bag for the night. I watched the stars through the door of the tunnel for some time before dozing off to sleep as the wind, as it had all day, roared outside my safe haven.

I awoke at 6:30 and checked the thermometer on my watch. Twenty-nine degrees. The sky above was an endless blue. It was quiet outside—the wind had disappeared, a welcome occurrence. I was hiking by 7:15, headed for Vaughn, almost thirty-one miles away. Between Fort Sumner and Vaughn, the land gradually climbs until it reaches over 6,000 feet. The climb is gained through a series of gradual ups and downs.

I was about halfway there when a gentleman and his two children pulled over in their pickup truck. He opened his truck door and handed me a half-gallon of water.

"Here, you will need this. Good luck," he said— and drove off.

I really didn't need the water, but didn't have much choice in the matter. It was a very kind gesture, and he was genuinely concerned for my welfare. How could I help but to stop and smile. I topped off my bottles then took a break to eat lunch and drink as much of the remaining water as possible. I dumped the rest out before securing the large plastic container onto my pack.

It was a perfect day, and the scenery that afternoon was majestic. I looked out to my north at Argonne Mesa and Mesa Leon. Between them, far into the distance, I could see a snow-covered mountain peak. I was beginning to learn what attracted people to this land of enchantment.

Despite the magnificent weather and scenery, I was again having a problem with my left foot. Not a blister this time, but a pain deep in my foot. I thought back to the injury that had driven Dodger from the trail in Texas and prayed that I would not meet a similar fate.

I spent the next several days watching the mountains appear and disappear along the north and south horizons, and waiting to see mountains to the west. That would signal that I was getting close to the end of the plains. The pain in my foot remained a constant discomfort, but I knew at that point that I would be able to continue.

I walked into Encino to discover the town had an eerie feel to it. I walked past several deserted houses that were somehow defying gravity, as their broken walls remained standing. I saw no people, just run down houses and run down cars. No dogs, no cats, just empty streets. I reached the west end of town and the only store. Here I found Mike and Jeff waiting for me. Inside, the store carried a few basic staples, but much like the town, its better days were behind it.

I was but a few days away from Allen's house in Mountainair. I called him to see if he might be able to shuttle me for a few days as I hiked from Encino into Mountainair. I could day hike this section, giving my tender foot a chance to rest. Allan agreed and Mike and Jeff offered to drive me into town to meet Allan. I spent that night at Allen's house in Mountainair.

Allan dropped me off in Encino at nine the next morning. It was cool and the wind was again blowing very hard, gusting well over forty miles per hour. The tumbleweeds bounced and flew down the road towards me as I got out of the car. There had been no wind at Allan's house, protected as it was by the mountains and trees.

As I donned my fleece top, Allan asked, "Are you sure you want to head out in this weather?"

"I think so," I unsurely replied, knowing I must.

"Well here, at least take my windbreaker. It will help you," he said, handing me his jacket.

Off I went, headfirst into the surging windstorm. Allan drove up about a mile and stopped to wait for me. When I reached the car he offered one last time, "Last chance. We can come back tomorrow."

"I'll be OK, but thanks," I reassured him.

"Well hey, my friend Jim will be passing through today, probably around noon. I told him to keep an eye out for you. You should not be hard to spot; I don't imagine there will be many hikers out here today," he said as if there were ever hikers on this road.

"That is good," I said, perking up. "That gives me an option. If the wind is too much, I can get out of it when Jim comes by, and I can still get nine or ten miles in without being in this brutal wind all day."

I headed on. Allan drove by and waved. I peered westward as his lights—and my shelter from the wind—vanished over the horizon. About four miles out of town, the wind just stopped, and the day's hike became much more pleasant.

Just before noon Jim pulled up, right on schedule. I decided to hike on, as the day had become so beautiful. Jim handed me a few bagels as we introduced ourselves. He quickly moved on to Allan's house, and I resumed walking.

As I crested a long climb, I saw a mountain on the western horizon. It was the mountain I had been looking for, for that mountain signified the end of the desert plains and the start of the southern Rockies. It was still thirty-five miles away, but I could see it.

I stopped on top of the ridge for a break to enjoy the day, the view, and the incredible happiness that ran through me. I was nearly across the plains!

The ridge top stood at 6,700 feet. The valley was nearly 300 feet below. I began the long slow decline, just smiling at the thought of soon seeing trees again, and of steams running through the forest.

That night was spent talking with Jim and Allan while poring over maps and taking in all of the information Allan had to offer. Before I left Mountainair, I would have a detailed route through western New Mexico and Arizona.

The next morning, I woke to the smell of bacon and coffee. What a wonderful odor in the morning! After breakfast, I returned to Route 60 and resumed. I had covered several miles when I reached a salt lake, the first of several in the area. These huge beds of salt were the only source of salt in northern New Mexico until well after 1900. The Pueblo Indians used the salt to barter with the Plains tribes to the east. As I stood there, I could see the snow-covered mountains near Albuquerque to my north. I suspected one was Sandia Peak, which stands over 10,000 feet high. Indeed, it was an incredible sight.

I reached the former pinto-bean farm region of Mountainair by early afternoon. The drought in the 1950s ended the farming days in the area, and today it is a quiet tourist town.

The next day, Jim drove me north to the Albuquerque airport to meet Nina. It would be good to spend a few days off, and to see Nina again. That evening Nina and I went to Historic Old Town Albuquerque and walked around. We enjoyed a wonderful dinner at The High Noon Restaurant. Built in 1875, the old building once housed a gambling casino and a popular brothel. The downtown area of Albuquerque has a special feel about it. Its past is alive, physically and spiritually.

After dinner, we drove out of town to the desert to look at the stars. Looking back down on Albuquerque, we could see the city lights shimmering across the valley a thousand feet below. The stars filled the clear, cold night sky above. It was a magical evening.

When I awoke the next morning, I was thirty-nine years old. I was alive and well: living, not just existing. I could ask no more from my first thirty-nine years. After enjoying the continental breakfast at the hotel, I talked Nina into driving to the top of the mountain that I had seen so many times while hiking: Sandia Peak.

We drove up the dirt back roads, in no great hurry. We drove and climbed, passing several patches of snow on our way up. We had reached nearly 9,000 feet when I saw a picnic area. I suggested that we take a picture together there, and Nina quickly agreed. She sat on a small stone wall, waiting for me to set up the camera. I set the timer and then the multi-picture option. Nina was all set for the picture, and I ran to her to beat the timer—then suddenly dropped onto one knee. There, among the beauty of the Sandia Mountains, amidst the glory of nature, I asked her tomarry me. Her face lit up in surprise and elation as she said repeatedly "Yes! Yes! YES!"

It was a special moment. We sat on the small stone wall hugging when Nina looked up at the tree behind us. There was a white blaze marking a trail, much like those that marked our beloved Appalachian Trail back east. We laughed heartily, both aglow with love and happiness.

We drove the rest of the way to Sandia Peak, our spirits as high as the 10,378—foot peak itself. We enjoyed lunch at the small restaurant on top before driving back to Albuquerque. Once in town, we stopped by a local jeweler to buy an engagement ring.

The weekend flew by, and we kept busy visiting the historic downtown, the mountains, and the Petroglyph National Monument, where we were able to hike and see the ancient carvings, some nearly 3,000 years old. A petroglyph is made by chipping away the rock's outer desert varnish, exposing a lighter grey rock underneath, leaving a lasting impression. These rocks are the silent keepers of ancient messages left by people who have long-since perished.

Our two nights in town were spent at the 200-year-old Hacienda Antigua Bed & Breakfast. The old place was charming, like a mansion to a hiker who had been on the trail, staying in dingy hotels for so many miles. The fireplace in the room had a soft, warm glow and set the mood for our entire stay.

All too soon, it was time for Nina to return to Louisiana, and me to continue west. I would be in Campo, California, soon and we would hike together. I dropped her off at the airport and then waited until my friends Mike and Jeff Smith picked me up to return me to Mountainair.

On our way, we stopped at the Quarai Pueblo ruins. The main chapel, nearly forty feet high, still stands as it slowly decays. Built in the early 1600s, it looks out of place in the lonely, arid plains.

The place commands reverence and I stood in awe, looking at the craftsmanship that went into building the massive cathedral. Each brick was hand-made of mud and straw, then baked in the sun. The construction was solid enough that it still stands today, ever so slowly baking and disintegrating back into the soil from where it rose up nearly four hundred years ago.

The main structure was the church and many small rooms were built alongside to serve as ceremonial rooms or housing for the priests. We walked the silent halls, passing from one chamber to the next—what a magnificent place.

We reached Mountainair around 5:30, and I bid Jeff and Mike farewell yet again. I did not expect to see them again.

With the long weekend behind me, I left Mountainair the next morning. It felt good to be hiking again, and the landscape west of town was dotted with juniper trees—or maybe "shrubs" would better describe them. It was good to see trees, to have some protection from the wind that had tortured me since I had entered Texas nearly five hundred miles back.

I reached another of the three Pueblo ruins late that morning, the Abo Ruins. From prehistoric times to the mid-17th century, Tompiro and Tiwa Pueblo Indians occupied the area. Early in the 17th century, the Spanish appeared, in search of silver and gold. They found no gold, but were given the duty of converting the natives to Christianity by the Pope. The Franciscan missionaries built these elaborate chapels, using the natives as laborers.

As I reached the porch of the visitors' center, Murt, the Forest Service Ranger, greeted me. He had a glass of water and a big smile for me. He had seen me coming. He was very knowledgeable and taught me a lot of the history. The missions were built in the 1620s. The one at Abo stands forty feet high. The Pueblos accepted the Spanish Franciscan missionaries and built the chapels under the direction of the Spanish. Originally, they were allowed to keep their native religion, but around 1650, the missionaries outlawed the Pueblo religion. The Pueblo Medicine Men were called devils and those caught practicing the native religion were severely punished.

The entire region was besieged with drought and widespread famine in the 1660s and 1670s. The natives blamed it on the Spanish for having outlawed their religion. The missions were finally abandoned during the 1670s. In 1680, the Pueblos rebelled, killing twenty-one priests and several hundred other Spaniards, driving them from New Mexico. They moved south to what is now El Paso and were absorbed by the native communities there. Forever lost, however, was their language and their homeland.

I left the historic site and turned off of Route 60. The next few days were spent hiking in the shadows of the Manzano Mountains to my north and Los Pinos Mountains and the Sevilleta National Wildlife Refuge to the southwest. I camped that night on the side of a hill, on a small, level ledge I found. It felt good to have silence again, to be off the highway and in the mountains among the trees.

I was packed and hiking by 8:30 the next morning and had only gone a few miles when a car pulled over. "Hi there, my name is Cathy Lee. Where ya off to on this beautiful morning?" She inquired.

"Well, I am cutting across the mountains, trying to get to Socorro," I replied.

"Well now, do ya have a map? Let me see that. My husband and I own a ranch just up the road a ways. If you take our road, it will save you a good ten miles. It is gated, but just go on through. Maybe I will see you later today. Do you need anything?"

"Well Mrs. Lee, I could use a little water if you have some."

"I always carry water," she said smiling as she handed me a bottle. "You have a good day now," she offered as she drove away.

Another mile up the road and I met a Mr. Sanchez. At seventy-five, he was still working the family ranch that he grew up on. His grandparents settled the land in the 1870s. He had driven to the end of the lane to put some mail into his mailbox. He sat in his decade-old truck, his rough hands holding onto the steering wheel, his weathered face peering at me through the open window. When he smiled, so did his eyes.

"Good morning sir." I opened.

"Well good morning," he replied as his cattle wandered around the open pasture, some of them eating the frozen cactus pods. I noticed one of them had a big piece of cactus stuck to its nose.

I looked in disbelief and asked, "They eat the cactus?"

"Why yeah, they eat anything they can find."

In our conversation, I learned about ranching in the west. I learned that it takes an entire section, 640 acres, to raise ten cattle. That is in a good year; in a drought year, you can expect six to eight cattle per section of land. The average ranch in New Mexico is about 40,000 acres, enough to raise 625 cattle.

We talked for nearly an hour when his great-granddaughter came out to tell him he had a phone call. He wished me well, then retreated to his house, and I resumed my ambling down the dirt lane. When Mr. Sanchez goes, so too will another family-owned farm. His children have no interest, and he expects they will sell it.

That afternoon I reached the Lee family Ranch. Just as Cathy had promised me, the road passed right through their horse corral. I quickly proceeded through the corral, and then set out across the rarely used dirt path into the mountains. I camped alone in a great valley, surrounded by the majestic mountains. I watched the sunset as I ate dinner in total silence. What a way to end the day.

The next morning I set out under gorgeous skies of blue and the temperature near fifty. The old farm lane I followed was not much more than a trail. I had only gone a few miles when the path ended at a windmill with several cattle milling about. I could go back and try to figure out where I made a wrong turn, or I could test my map and compass skills. I felt adventurous and chose the latter. I knew if all else failed, I could just go west and I would eventually hit the Rio Grande River and civilization.

The plant life on this side of Mountainair was incredibly different from that on the east side. While it is still an extremely arid ecosystem, there is enough moisture to support a sparse mixture of juniper, cactus, short grasses, and several other small grassy and thorny plants. It also supports songbirds, and I hiked along enjoying their songs as they flittered about me.

I shot my bearing and headed for a distant mountain. I figured when I reached the mountain I would go around its west side. I kept an eye on my GPS and map. As I got close, they disagreed with my original assessment. Should I trust my instinct or my tools? I chose the latter and hiked around the east side instead. I hiked in and around the mountains and eventually found the dirt road I was looking for. A few miles later, I crested a hill to discover the rich green Oasis of the Rio Grande valley below me. I pushed on into the town of Escondida, and crossed the Rio Grande River. I then headed south, paralleling I-25 into Socorro.

Socorro is close to the White Sands Missile Range, where the first atomic bomb was detonated in 1945. There were announcements given on the radio several times warning of a test at the site for early the next week. I was glad I'd be well west of the area by then.

The next day, I left Socorro and headed for Magdalena. I could walk the road around, or take a shortcut through the Cibola National Forest and the Magdalena Mountains, saving a few miles and allowing me some more time in the mountains. I had packed food for lunch and had enough water to get me to town. I cut off Route 60 again and headed towards the mountain. The elevation in the valley was about 6,000 feet.

My first misconception was that going over the mountain would be a shortcut. On the map, it appears shorter, but the map does not consider elevation gain; it assumes the land is flat. I knew this, but for some reason it didn't register.

I headed off on Forest Road 505, looking for Forest Road 505A. 505A, according to my map, is the only turn off 505; it shouldn't have been hard to find.

I soon reached a "T" in the road; it sure looked like my route, but it was not marked. The Forest Service is usually very good about marking their roads, but I decided to follow it anyhow. About a half mile up the road I passed a running windmill—a water source. I decided I had plenty of water to get me across the mountain, so I marked its location on my GPS and passed it up. I climbed up to about 7,500 feet, where the road suddenly stopped. Instead of turning around, I continued to climb up, bushwhacking through the dense pine trees and undergrowth. I climbed another 2,100 feet and could go no more. The undergrowth was too thick. I turned and looked down at the plains below me. I could see Route 60 several miles out, still it felt good to be on a mountain again, even if I wasn't sure where exactly on the mountain I was.

As I explored the mountains from my perch, I noticed a road down in the valley to my north. That must have been the road I wanted. How could I have missed it? I scrambled down the scree on the north side of the mountain, sliding and holding on to anything I could as I went.

I dropped 1,000 feet, all the way back down to 6,500 feet elevation, to the road I had seen. From here I again began to climb. I checked my watch and realized it was nearly five o'clock.; daylight would soon be an issue.

I thought, "If I can just make it to the summit by dark, I will be able to night-hike into town." After climbing 1,500 feet, to about 8,000 feet elevation, the road, just like the first one, abruptly ended.

It was now 5:45. I had 45 minutes of daylight and was very low on water. I had been rationing my water, sipping just enough to wet my mouth. After several bad decisions, I knew it was imperative that I make a good decision now.

I needed more water. I decided to turn around and head back to the windmill and then to Forest Service Road 505. Using my GPS, I had little trouble finding the windmill. When I arrived, the wind that had been blowing earlier had ceased. There was no more flowing water. All that was available was the water in the cattle pond. I didn't have a filter with me, and opted to not fill my bottle with the black water from the pond.

I reached Forest Service Road 505 again at 6:30. I would follow it northwest, and it would eventually bring me back out onto Route 60. I was still 12 miles from town this way, but it was the best option I had left.

Off I went, night hiking along the forest road. The sky was clear, and the moonlight was all I needed to find my way. Around 7:15, I hit a crossroad with another windmill, and a sign. The windmill was old and out of service, and the sign said Forest Road 505A--the road I had spent all afternoon looking for.

I was nearly out of water. If I continued back down to Route 60, I would never make town tonight. If I could just make it over this mountain, I thought, I could make it down the other side to town. I decided to take Forest Road 505A up the mountain. It was shorter, but more strenuous

and at that point, the shortest distance was the best. I could
not afford to get lost again.

I climbed Magdalena Mountain for a third time.
Up, up, up I climbed the very rugged steep mountain road.
I soon ran out of water and began to question my decision.
I was not afraid I might die or anything that extreme; it was
more a matter of the self-inflicted discomfort I was about to
suffer.

At 8:15, I found a snow bank. I ate some snow just
to wet my mouth. I looked at my GPS. I was at 8,100 feet
elevation, still well below the summit. I was fatigued,
hungry, and thirsty. It was time to make another good
decision. I decided camp on the road. The mountain
would still be here in the morning.

I took my two water bottles and filled them with
snow, packing them full. I lay out my Thermarest sleeping
pad between the rocks on the road and then my sleeping
bag. I climbed in with the two very cold water bottles. I
would use my body heat as I slept to melt the icy snow. I
knew it took a lot of snow to make a little water, but
hopefully this would make enough to get me over the
mountain.

I had only some cheese and a Snickers bar for food
and opted to not eat because I had no water to wash it
down. I drifted off to sleep as I looked at the millions of
stars above. The moon was still bright and shined over me
like a nightlight in a kid's bedroom. It was time for rest.

I awoke to a flat sleeping pad. I must have missed a
sharp rock in the dark. The good news was that my little
water-making project was a success; I had about two thirds
of a quart of water. Not enough to swim in, but certainly
enough to allow me to reach town, if I didn't get misplaced

again. The mountain was not sympathetic, however, and
the morning climb to the summit was strenuous, to say the
least. I reached the top around 8:30 at 9,500 feet elevation.
Wow, what a view—but no sign of town. I was at yet
another crossroad, and there was another small peak
between town and me. Which road do I take around the
peak, I thought. I dropped my pack and ran northeast on
the road for about a quarter mile. I soon decided that was
the wrong way, so I returned to my pack and went around
the last peak going northwest. As I came around it, I could
see town below me. It was a peaceful view, and I was
certainly glad to see it. I could also see a church steeple
about halfway down the mountain. I rested on top for a
while, enjoying the view and the sight of town.

I eventually reached the church I had seen. I
stopped to rest, and discovered that I was in the ghost town
of Kelly, New Mexico. From the 1860s through the 1890s,
Kelly had been one of the most prosperous mining towns in
all of New Mexico. Now there are just old broken-down
foundations and the church, which still stands. The mine is
evidently open for tourists in the summer, but I chose not to
go into it. I took a few pictures and continued my descent
down the dusty dirt road into Magdalena.

I ran out of water about a mile before I got to town.
I had not eaten in twenty-six hours, but amazingly enough I
didn't feel hungry. I got a room and showered before
heading down the street to get some lunch, knowing I
needed to eat—hungry or not. I then gathered my laundry
and put it in at the local Laundromat. Next door was the
Golden Spur Saloon. I retreated to the hospitality of the
place to enjoy a cold beer. I met many of the local folks
including Pockets, Sissy, and Allen. We had a wonderful
afternoon swapping stories and laughing. Allen invited me

to his house for dinner where I met his wife, Janice, and their granddaughter. We grilled up a few steaks and talked about adobe brick construction methods, and life in the small town of Magdalena.

The population here is just 1,200 and the main jobs are ranching and the Very Large Array (VLA), which I would pass in a few days. For nearly a century, from 1885 to 1971, there was a 125-mile-long livestock route called the Magdalena Livestock Driveway. It ran from Springerville, Arizona, to Magdalena, where the railroad was. The peak year was 1919, when 150,000 sheep and 21,600 cattle were driven along this route. In the 1930s, the Civilian Conservation Corps fenced the entire route and drilled water wells every ten miles. The route finally gave way to trucking; the last portion closed in November 1971.

A few days later I found myself approaching the Plains of San Agustin and the VLA. Thousands of years ago a huge lake filled this valley. I bet it was spectacular. Today the 7,000-foot high plains are home to the VLA. The VLA is one of two National Radio Astronomy Observatories. It is one of the world's premier astronomical radio observatories. It is made up of twenty-seven radio antennas in a Y-shaped pattern, reaching into the heavens, taking sound pictures of the universe. Each antenna is eighty-one feet wide. Data is gathered from each dish and combined electronically, which then improves the resolution to that of an antenna twenty-two miles across. Scientists come from around the globe to do research and deep-space experiments. The site has also been in many films.

The plains stretch for about eighteen miles east-to-west and are surrounded on all sides by mountains. The valley is absolutely barren, an ideal place for the VLA, but

it made for a challenging walk on a cold windy day. I
stopped just short of the tree line and put on my long pants,
gloves, and windproof coat. I was soon out of the safety of
the trees, facing the cold, relentless wind. I hiked a mile or
so and realized I was losing the battle with the wind. I
stopped again, unpacked my pack, and added my rain pants
and fleece hat to my wardrobe. This did the trick, and I
stayed warm the rest of the way across.

I finally reached the end of the San Agustin Plains,
and the warmth and safety of the trees and mountains.
Here, nestled in the hills, is the small town of Datil. Started
as a watering hole for cowboys and cattle along the stock
trail, today it is a very small community with one
store/motel/restaurant. It was my supply point, as I'd left
Magdalena with enough food to get me there. I would
never have dreamed that the town shuts down on Sunday—
everything, even the motel. Granted, I didn't ask the fine
folks back in Magdalena, but I had never heard of a motel
shutting down every Sunday.

Well there I was, hungry again. I could slide into
the mountains and camp, and return in the morning to eat,
supply and hit the trail. I noticed a pay phone across the
street at the post office, so I walked over to check my
email.

I received word from a friend that my old college
roommate's brother had passed away. We had known each
other since kindergarten, growing up just a few houses
apart. I needed to go home, but how could I do that? I was
in Datil, New Mexico and the whole town was closed.
Fortunately, I had Allen's phone number back in
Magdalena. I called him and he came to get me.

I checked into the Western Hotel and called Nina to
see if she could find me a flight. I made another call to

Mike and Jeff Smith in Albuquerque to see if there was any way they could get me to the airport, a hundred miles away in Albuquerque. Nina found a flight to Cleveland Ohio, and Jeff and Mike pledged their support. The last issue was getting from Cleveland back to Steubenville. I called another friend who lives near Cleveland, and he said he could pick me up.

It is important to keep all things in perspective. The mountains would still be there. My friends' time of need for love and support was now.

After four unexpected days away from the trail, I returned. If not for the kindness of so many, I never would have made it. Mike and Jeff dropped me off in Datil around 12:30 and wished me well one more time.

I resumed my walk west, ominous dark clouds looming on the horizon ahead of me. I was sure that eventually I would get wet, but the storm stayed to my north. I watched as the clouds engulfed the mountains in that direction. I climbed steadily on and stayed dry.

At dusk, I reached the Western Continental Divide at 7,800 feet elevation. I pitched my tent behind a small grove of trees. All the rivers and streams east of here and west of the Eastern Continental Divide flow into the Gulf of Mexico, everything west of here flows into the Pacific Ocean.

I was up and gone early the next morning, hiking the last mile into Pie Town and the Pio-O-Neer Café in time for a good cup of coffee and breakfast. When in Pie Town, you must eat pie, even if you're only in town for breakfast!

Pie Town got its name in the late 1800s. A cowboy decided to start ranching there, but his ranching skills left something to be desired. He then opened a small store and cafe to serve the other ranchers passing through. His pies became famous, and folks called the stop Pie Town. When it came time to get a post office, the government wanted a new name, but the residents insisted on keeping the name. Pie Town. The Continental Divide Trail passes through, and after breakfast I crossed over it, another milestone in my westward journey.

My day ended in Quemado, my last supply point in New Mexico. I would soon notch another state on my slate, as Springerville, Arizona was only forty-nine miles west.

After a quiet night alone in Quemado, I climbed out of town, with my pack laden with twelve pounds of water plus food for two days. I slowly walked the long, gradual ridge and was soon on top, crossing the plateau. The day began to heat up, and so did the road. The temperature reached the mid-80s by early afternoon, and I felt the effects of the heat all day. It had been a long time since I had been exposed to the hot sun. As I hiked, my left foot blistered in eight different places, including the arch of my foot. I had never heard of someone blistering the arch of their foot, but sure enough, I had managed to do so.

I stopped whenever I needed to apply first aid to my beaten foot, but that was it. I just kept moving. Finally around 3:30, I stopped for a reprieve from the scorching heat. I went under a bridge, where the shade gave me instant relief. I decided to cook dinner and relax. While I was cooking, a few clouds moved into the area, a welcome sight as they would protect me from the direct sunlight that had tortured me all day. I could see the next mountain, complete with trees, ahead of me. My goal was to reach them.

Around sunset, I discovered the "town" of Red Hill. I learned why it is not listed on the maps. There are two buildings there: a realtor's office, and the realtor's house.

As soon as the sun set, my hands got cold. It was not cold out, the temperature in the upper fifties, but my hands were like ice. I hiked another mile and found a bridge I could camp underneath. I was worn from the day's hike and decided I would not make it to the trees I had been watching throughout the day.

When I quit hiking and climbed under the bridge, I cooled off very quickly. I was shivering uncontrollably. I quickly rolled out my Thermarest and my fifteen-degree down sleeping bag, and crawled inside. I zipped it all the way up, sure I would be warm in no time. I shivered for nearly an hour.

Eventually I did warm up, but I knew something was terribly wrong with me. Perhaps I had a slight case of heat exhaustion. That night I stayed very warm, even sleeping much of the night with the bag unzipped because it was so warm.

My sleeping pad kept going flat, damaged from my night on the rocks atop Magdalena Mountain. I woke several times through the night and blew it back up. When I awoke at sunrise my knees hurt, the bottom of my feet hurt, and all my muscles were sore. My whole body ached. My mind was sluggish and I was worried I may have the flu. Perhaps the flat sleeping pad was the reason I hurt so badly; perhaps it was from the heat exhaustion I had suffered. It didn't matter; I had to walk, as I had water for only one more day.

I moved along as best I could, in search of the Arizona state line. I reached it around 11:30 and stopped to celebrate. I felt terrible, and I was still thirteen miles from town. I had force-marched ten and a half miles, promising myself I could have a break when I got to the state line.

I stopped and took a few uninspired pictures, then hobbled on another quarter-mile to a grassy spot beside the road. Off came my shoes, and I lay back to rest. I ate a Snickers bar and took some Ibuprofen, better known as Vitamin I in the hiking community. I then duct-taped my battered left little toe and gave myself a foot massage. Vitamin I Snickers and duct tape—if that doesn't make me feel better, I figured, I am in trouble.

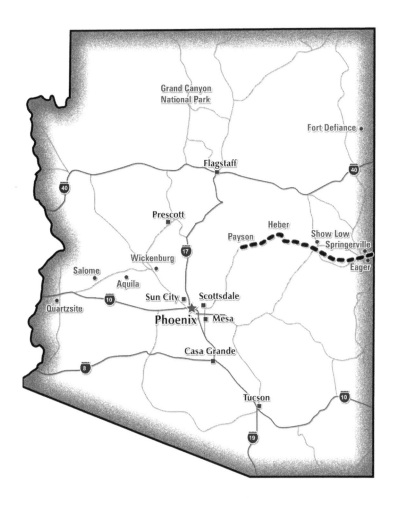

Arizona

My sugar high along with the small victory of
seeing the state line, lifted my spirits and eased my pain. I
managed to reach Springerville by mid-afternoon and was
feeling better about myself. I was surprised to find two
towns in this beautiful desert valley: Springerville and
Eagar. Curious as I was, I asked several of the local people
how this came to be.

In the late 1800s, Springerville was full of outlaws,
horse thieves and such. Harry Springer moved into the
then-unnamed town in the fall of 1875, and established a
store near the Little Colorado River. It was aptly named
Springer's Store. He made the mistake of trusting the
outlaws and allowed then to buy on credit. In less than a
year, he was broke and on his way out of town. When it
came time to name the town, the townsfolk found his
misfortune humorous, so they named the town after him.

In 1876, the Becker Brothers also started a store in
Springerville. There were literally no roads leading to
Springerville at the time. For the store to re-supply it
required a sixty-day round trip to Albuquerque. They used
ox-pulled wagons until about 1890, when they upgraded to
teams of horses and mules. Finally, in 1895, a rail line was
finished to nearby Magdalena, making the re-supply effort
much simpler.

Around this time, the Mormon community of Eagar was settled adjacent to Springerville. The Mormons loved the beautiful valley but wanted nothing to do with the outlaws who frequented Springerville, which is why they started their own town right next door.

I enjoyed a quiet night in the now domestic town before hiking on towards the White Mountains. On my way, I watched several antelope gallop gracefully across the immense open fields. I passed several small streams, each gurgling down the hills as I climbed. I reached Forest Service Road 117 shortly after noon and headed into Apache National Forest. I spent the next twenty-eight hours alone, not seeing another person, not even a passing car.

I steadily climbed, hiking between the patches of snow above 9,000 feet. The day was beautiful, and I was immersed in a feeling of absolute freedom. I thought of Nina coming to hike with me soon and was elated to think I would soon get to share this magnificent journey with her.

This Arizona was very different than the picture I had in my mind before seeing it for myself. I had pictured brown desert with cactus everywhere. This place was green, dominated by one of the largest stands of ponderosa pines on earth. The still-bare aspen mixed in, their white bark in stark contrast to that of the pine. The ground was coming alive as spring flowers began to arrive. The mountains were simply majestic.

I camped in a small meadow, the surrounding mountains rising up far above the 8,600-foot elevation where my tent was pitched. I was far away from anything and anyone. I lay in the open grass and watched the stars appear in the night sky, one by one. I gazed endlessly, enjoying the quietness and serenity of the place.

I had barely left my campsite the next morning when I jumped a flock of turkeys. There were several young ones, and they ran as quick as their short little legs would allow, following mom to safety.

Later in the morning, I crossed over from Apache to Sitgreaves National Forest. These two national forests comprise nearly two million acres. Just west is Tonto National Forest, which contains an additional three million acres. The US government and the Native Americans, in the form of reservations, own nearly 89% of all Arizona land. That leaves only 11% of the land to private owners.

It was nearly noon when I met two men building a fence. I assumed they were building it to keep cattle in for summer grazing. I was wrong. I learned they are building this fence to keep the cattle out, to provide grazing land for the deer and elk. It was a project coordinated between the National Forest Service and the National Turkey Federation. The National Turkey Federation has long been proactive in restoring and developing wildlife habitat, not only for turkey, but for other species as well.

We chatted for some time before I pressed on. Shortly afterwards I saw two elk, my first ever. They were not very close and ran when they heard me, but I got to see them. I sauntered down the dirt road, enjoying my time in the forest. No sooner had I gotten back into a good rhythm when a forest ranger pulled up beside me. He wanted to make sure I was OK. I had only one question for him, the same question I had for the past month:

"How is the water supply?"

"Well you know, I have been here for ten years or so, and I have never seen it so dry. Springs that usually run until late in the summer are already dry. We are very concerned that, by summer, there will be very few watering holes for the wildlife."

"Just down the road another mile or so is a campground. Is the spring there running?" I asked.

"Well, I think it is, but it is well over a mile off the road. You need a little water?" he offered.

"Well now if you have some extra I would certainly take it off your hands. It would save me the two-mile round trip. Thank you, sir"

I reached the town of Pine-Top around five and stopped at the Lion's Den for a world-famous hamburger and a cold one. When you walk into a place with a backpack on, everyone is your friend. They are all curious as to why you brought it in with you, where your car is, and how far you are going. This was no exception, and I quickly got into a good conversation.

The fellow next to me was named Willie, and he was the supervisor of a construction company. We talked for some time before he asked me where I planned to spend the night. He then told me that two of his employees had gone home, so he had an extra hotel room that was paid for, but empty. He handed me the key, saying someone may as well get some use from it. Incredible. Thanks so much, Willie.

My left little toe had been hurting for several days. It constantly rubbed against the side of my shoe, and by the end of the day it was cut open and bleeding. I had limped into camp the past several nights. The shoes had barely five hundred miles on them and were not worn out. I thought my feet might be growing. I learned there were stores near Show Low where I might find a larger pair.

The next day I did find a store and was able to get new shoes, as well as replace my worn sleeping pad. I made it to town and was walking down the sidewalk, minding my own business, when a car pulled into the parking lot next to me.

The window came down. "Is that a Kelty Cloud?" was the question.

Now, there are many packs out there, but the Kelty Cloud is different. It is white and is the only pack I know of that is white. It is also very expensive, and a common hobo would not have one. Hence, I regarded myself as an upscale hobo. The driver knew by my pack that I was doing something serious.

Feeling like I was in a commercial I replied, "Why, yes it is."

"Well hi there, my name is Howard Jones. Do you like it? I have one too, but it really doesn't fit my needs," he went on.

Our conversation continued for a few minutes, talking about hiking and mountain climbing, as Howard is a mountain climber. I gave him one of my business cards before he left, and then I headed back down the road. I had only gone about a half mile when he returned.

"Hey, I called my wife and she said I am allowed to bring home a stranger. Up for a free meal and a warm bed?" he happily offered.

It took me no time to accept an offer like that, and we were soon at his house. I quickly showered and threw in some laundry. Soon I had clean socks—little victories. As we talked more, I learned that Howard, like me, was once employed by corporate America. He left that to start his own business, developing software for real estate. I also learned just how much of a mountain climber he is. He had recently climbed Cerro Aconcagua in Argentina. The 22,841-foot mountain is the highest peak outside of the Himalayan Mountains. He has also climbed Mount Elbrus in Russia, the highest mountain in Europe at 18,481 feet, and Kilimanjaro in Africa, a 19,344-foot challenge, as well as Mount Rainer, Mount Whitney, and Mount Hood.

His wife Liz came home a bit later and prepared a sumptuous salmon dinner. The three of us sat and talked until almost nine, swapping stories of our adventures.

I awoke at 6:30, well-rested and full of energy. I sat in my room and wrote several emails before emerging around seven. Howard and Liz had just returned from their morning walk. Liz cooked a delicious scrambled-egg dish, while Howard shared his journal with me of the recent climb in Argentina. Climbing to 23,000 feet is certainly a different challenge than hiking.

In the northeast United States, there is the 4,000-foot club where members try to climb each of the fifty or so mountains there above 4,000 feet. In Colorado is the fourteeners club, where you try to climb all of the 14,000+-foot peaks there. Then there is the seven peaks club. You climb the highest peak on each continent. There are only about seventy-five people in it. Howard plans to climb Denali in Alaska soon, giving him four of the seven.

The morning rain stopped, and I headed out around ten. After bidding good-bye I headed towards town to get supplies for the next few days.

Once I was packed and standing at the edge of town, the rains returned. I donned my pack cover and raincoat, and then hoisted the pack laden with fourteen pounds of food and water onto my back and headed west.

The western sky was quickly transformed from a soft gray to an intimidating black.

I stood there listening to the thunder and looking at the motels all around me. I quickly debated if I should hike on or seek refuge. I thought, heck I am in town, safe and dry. Does it make any sense to walk out in a thunderstorm? With that bit of logic established, I walked out of town. The weatherman had said the chance of rain was only twenty percent, so perhaps this was just a passing shower.

It started as a light drizzle, and then it stopped. The sun returned and I was soon hot in my raincoat, so I stopped again to take it back off. I finally reached the dirt forest road at 1 PM, still dry and glad I had chosen to hike.

Never, ever, ever trust a weatherman. At 1:30, everything changed. It didn't rain—it hailed. I quickly put my raincoat back on in an attempt to protect myself from the missiles of ice. It hailed for a solid five minutes then abruptly stopped. The world around me turned dead silent—no wind—no birds—no nothing. Silence.

I had a feeling that the worst was yet to come, so I unpacked my pack and put my tent within easy reach. I also put my rain pants and rain gloves in the top. No sooner did I get everything back in my pack when the rain began in earnest. I unpacked the pack and put my rain clothes on yet again. The rain fell straight down, a solid two-hour drenching, a blessing for the drought-stricken mountains.

I soon discovered that dirt roads are not the best surface to hike on in a rainstorm. My brand-new shoes were not new for long. With every step, I gathered more mud on the bottom of each shoe, making me taller, and each step more laborious. Each shoe easily weighed four pounds, and I stopped repeatedly to scrape the mud off. Travel was slow, but I kept plodding along.

Finally, late in the afternoon the rains ceased. The temperature had dropped considerably, and the sky remained gloomy. It had been good to see the rain, perhaps it would help to relieve some of the stress the current drought had produced. I could have done without the muddy road, but sometimes I guess you have to walk down a muddy road.

About five-thirty, the skies again let loose, this time in the form of a biting cold drizzle. I hiked until dusk, knowing I would never make as many miles as I had planned. My goal had been to get far enough to allow me to make it to town the next day. I had to make town, or I would run out of water.

Just as I found a tent site, the rains ceded yet again. I took the opportunity to quickly cook dinner and set up camp and was in my tent by seven, dry and warm.

As I was falling asleep, I could hear the pitter-patter of rain on the tent roof, the first rain my new tent had seen in nearly 1,000 miles of hiking. I awoke around one to find the tent roof sagging, nearly touching my face. It was covered with wet, heavy snow. I pushed on the ceiling of the tent, forcing the snow to slide off, and then quickly fell back asleep in my toasty-warm sleeping bag.

At first light, I peered out of my tent. It was still snowing. I certainly had not planned on seeing snow in Arizona. I again reached up and cleaned the roof of the tent, giving relief to the strained fabric. I lay in the tent, thinking about how muddy that road must be. I would never make it the twenty-two miles to town on that road.

I packed my gear while sitting inside my tent, then got out in the snow and packed my tent into the outer pocket of my pack. I decided to hike out of the forest and onto the main road when I reached the next crossing. This would get me off the muddy forest road, and allow me to make positive progress.

I met two forest rangers out patrolling. As we spoke, they told me about the General George Crook National Scenic Trail. I had seen parts of it on my map, but the detail for it was sketchy. They informed me I was nearly standing on it, and assured me it would be a pleasant walk, even wet.

General George Crook, considered the Army's greatest Indian fighter, was born in Ohio in 1828. He graduated from West Point near the bottom of his class in 1852. He had a deep respect for the Native Americans and carried that respect with him in all of his dealings with them, be it fighting or negotiating. After serving in Indian wars in several states, as well as the in Civil War, he returned to Arizona in 1882. His mission was to put the Apache back on their reservations. The next four years were spent chasing and fighting Geronimo. Crook and his forces cornered Geronimo and his band of followers time and time again; and time after time, they watched helplessly as they escaped into their rugged mountain strongholds. In 1886, Crook was relieved of command by General Nelson A. Miles. The famous Lakota Chief, Red Cloud, said of George Crook, "…he never lied to us. His words gave the people hope." General George Crook died on March 2, 1890.

Finally tired of running, Geronimo's band of sixteen warriors, twelve women, and six children surrendered later that year. The surrender marked the end of the Indian wars in the United States. Geronimo and his followers were exiled to Florida. He died on Feb. 17, 1909, still listed as a prisoner of war. He was buried in the Apache Cemetery at Fort Sill, Oklahoma, having never returned to his homeland.

I began down the George Crook Trail, and found the hiking much more to my liking. The whole trail runs 128 miles, and parallels the road that General Crook built to supply the forts in the area. I followed it all the way to the edge of the town of Heber, where I spent the night.

The next morning, I headed south on Black Canyon Road, through the last vestiges of rundown houses and cluttered yards on the outskirts of Heber. I quickly left town behind and was back in Sitgreaves National Forest.

I stopped several times to climb the steep side trails to see some of the hundreds of petroglyphs that abound in the Black Canyon area. I sat in awe, amazed at the fact that 3,000 years ago, a man sat here with a rock and chisel, making these drawings of people, insects, and animals. The petroglyphs have weathered extremely well, and I am sure they tell a story somehow. It is easy to see why people chose Black Canyon to live; it is beautiful, with tall pines and a big open canyon between the mountain walls to the east and west.

Late that afternoon, I reached the small Baca Family Cemetery. The Baca Family homesteaded this land in the 1880s; about the time that General George Crook was building the road between Fort Apache and Fort Prescott. They had a son and six daughters before Mr. Baca passed away. Their son was fifteen at the time and became head of the household. Single women were scarce in the Arizona Territory, and with six young women, suitors frequented the house.

Mrs. Baca raised the family in the land she loved. She befriended the Apache natives, and they protected her. Today, in the silence of a million acres of national forest, sits the privately owned graveyard of the Baca family. The place has a profound energy to it, a feeling of triumph, of happiness, of fulfillment.

I pressed on and climbed out of the beautiful valley, reaching Black Canyon Lake around three. The water level at the lake was down, yet another byproduct of the drought that continued to torture the already-arid mountains. I again encountered the George Crook Trail and followed it the remaining four miles into Forest Lakes.

There was only one place to stay in the small town of Forest Lakes. I checked in, only to learn that the restaurant was closed until May and that the only store in town had closed for the evening. This was not good news, as I always planned to get the night's meal in town when I arrived. I did not carry extra food. The couple running the place was originally from Ohio, and we soon got to chatting.

They were overwhelmed at the thought of me walking all the way from Ohio. They had a small pantry of food just for such an occasion and gave me a burrito, some crackers, and a can of Spam to enjoy for dinner.

I wish I weren't so dependent on towns for water, but there was not much water in the wilderness. To complicate matters, I didn't know the area well enough to know what springs I could count on. The nights that I stayed in hotels were spent talking with Nina, as we planned for our time together along the Pacific Crest Trail. That night's talk was different however, as Nina informed me her grandmother had fallen very ill, and she did not think she would be able to hike with me over the summer.

My time in the mountains was quickly ending, and the next day I crossed over Arizona's other geological wonder, the Mogollon Rim. I reached the edge of the rim, and the visitor center. The rim marks the southern end of the Colorado Plateau. It is an abrupt ending and in places drops 2,000 feet. General Crook's road was built along the edge of the rim, and much of the route is still in use today as a Forest Service road.

The visitors center was not open for the season yet, so I sat and peered out from the porch at the vast wilderness below the rim. It was time to leave the high mountains and begin working my way to the desert on the valley floor, over 6,000 feet below.

My mind wandered as I descended. Did I want to spend the summer hiking without Nina? I became depressed. I made my way down to the town of Christopher Creek and stopped at the local tavern/restaurant for dinner. I enjoyed the company of several of the local folks, but I felt alone. After dinner, I walked down to my room and went to sleep, hoping I would feel better in the morning.

I met the friends I had made the night before, Bob and Larry, for breakfast. They mentioned my little adventure to Barbara, our morning waitress, and she wanted to hear all about it. Soon Bob and Larry finished their breakfast and were off to work. Olive, the restaurant owner, and her daughter Lynn replaced them at the table. We enjoyed a morning cup of coffee while talking of adventures. Lynn has cycled extensively throughout the world. She was quite interested in my adventure, and in short order decided it was newsworthy. She made a phone call, and I was all set to do a newspaper interview when I reached Payson the next day.

I headed on after breakfast, having enjoyed the fellowship and company. It was too short, however, and I longed to have deeper fellowship—to have someone to talk with daily.

The road out of town was a challenge, as often there was no berm at all. The road twisted up and between the hills, giving me a very limited viewing distance as well. I kept moving, staying extremely attentive to oncoming traffic. Repeatedly I would stop and step off the road into the relative safety of the rough, narrow piece of land that clung to the edge of the hill.

I reached the small town of Star Valley, just four miles east of Payson. I stopped. I had hiked eighteen miles already, and my depression was getting worse. I did not feel like hiking on alone. I got a room and called Nina. I had looked forward to her joining me; I was not adjusting to the idea of hiking the Pacific Crest Trail alone very well at all. Nina encouraged me to get out there and continue on. It was my dream, and I must not shortchange myself.

The next day brought an uneventful four-mile walk into Payson. On the edge of town, I stopped at the National Forest Ranger Station to let them know I would be in the Mazatal Wilderness for a few days. They told me to call the sheriff, as they do not do rescues.

I was on into town and to yet another hotel. I immediately called Nina.

"Is there any way you can come and join me?" I pleaded.

"I wish I could, I have been looking forward to it, but there is just no way. I have to get a lot of dental work done and my grandmother is on her deathbed. I can't do it."

We hung up, and a million thoughts raced through my mind. I had been struggling lately with loneliness on two levels. The first was the simple loneliness of not having any companionship for 1,200 of the last 1,400 miles. I found myself going to town at every chance, just to chat with someone. Even with that, there was no camaraderie, merely a short hello and then on. The other loneliness was being away from Nina. I had looked forward to spending the summer hiking with her, and now this was no longer a possibility.

I had three options: to go on and hike alone to the Pacific Crest Trail, meet other hikers there and enjoy a good summer on the trail, without Nina; to take the money I had saved and offer to cover Nina's expenses for hiking so that we could enjoy the Pacific Crest Trail together; or to put the hike on hold, go home and start life with Nina, and possibly return someday to continue the trek. However, the third option meant possibly never seeing Payson, Arizona again.

When I started this journey, I had not planned to fall in love, but I had. The desire to go on alone was gone, and I decided to go back east for the summer. I could have paid her way, but the stock market had been in a months-long slump and my portfolio was greatly affected. I was hopeful that things would work out and I would return . . . someday.

"Nina. I am coming home."

"Dan, you can't come home. You have to go on!"

"I said when I started I don't need anyone's permission to start, I don't need permission to stop. I am coming home. I have enjoyed 2,700 beautiful miles of America. I am going to do a newspaper interview in the morning and then head home. I will see you soon."

The next morning I interviewed with Beth Geth for the *Payson Roundup*, then bought a newspaper and a car. All too quickly, I was on my way back east.

I had hiked through the fall and winter, and spring was just arriving. I had met hundreds of wonderful people and had experienced the eastern hardwood forest, the southern pine forest and swamps, the Great Plains and finally the southern Rockies. It was time for me to go home, at least for now.

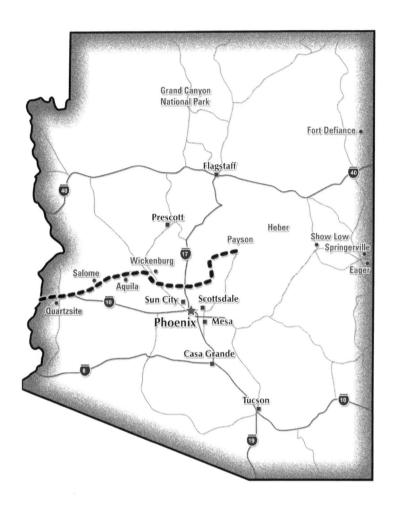

Arizona Revisited

The summer was spent with Nina, traveling up and down the East Coast, visiting friends, hiking, and writing. She had encouraged me to return to finish my walk across the country as soon as the desert cooled off enough. Yes, I had unfinished business, and the time had come to return to Payson. I decided to change the route to take me north from Payson through the Grand Canyon and Zion National Park before turning south and heading towards San Diego.

My friend Eb Eberhart, known as Nimblewill Nomad in the hiking community, was also hiking cross-country. He had left from Cape Hatteras, North Carolina several months earlier. Our paths would cross in western Arizona.

With the 2,250-mile journey in my van complete, I found myself sitting again at the Days Inn in Payson, the same Days Inn where I had stayed in April. I was tired from five days in the car and had not slept particularly well. With breakfast behind me, I drove to my friend Beth's house to drop off my van. We talked a few minutes, and then she drove me back to the Days Inn. After a thank you and a good-bye to her, I walked into the motel to get my pack. As I was walking down the hall, the manager noticed me and immediately recognized me. He was excited to see I had returned and wished me well.

The day was cool, with white puffy clouds floating above, intermixed with dark black clouds and spots of deep blue sky. I walked strongly for most of the day—hiking the Long Trail in Vermont with Nina just before returning had been a good idea. Late in the afternoon however, my knees began to hurt. Walking on the pavement was wearing me out. I stopped to rest several times in the last eight miles, after hiking the first eight non-stop.

I reached the small village of Pine and stopped at the local restaurant for dinner, then walked on to discover a small RV park with a cabin for rent.

"Which way ya going?" asked the owner.

"I am headed north on the Arizona Trail, all the way to Utah," I confidently replied.

"Well you're a braver man than me, there ain't no water on that trail," he replied.

"I have a small guide here. It says there are cattle tanks that the springs feed, and I figure they will have water."

"Been dry for months. This drought is bad, I'm telling ya."

I pored over my maps that night. Would I be ok? Being in the desert is one thing, but being in the desert during a drought is another. After thinking about it, I decided to continue with my planned route.

The next morning took me off the road and onto the Pine Canyon Trail, which would lead me to the Arizona Trail some ten miles away, back on the top of the Mogollon Rim. My pack was heavy, as if I had filled it with rocks. The seven quarts of water and several days of food were a burden I had not encountered in some time. I had walked about four miles when I reached my first trail junction. One trail marked "Johnson Canyon" split away and climbed steeply up the mountainside. My map did not show Johnson Canyon. As a matter of fact, my map did not show this junction at all. Furthermore, the trail sign did not mention what trail went straight, and I was unsure which way to go.

What I *did* know was I had to climb to reach the top of the Mogollon Rim again. I chose to hike up Johnson Canyon, because it went uphill. All was fine until the trail abruptly ended, much like the roads on Magdalena Mountain back in New Mexico. I stopped and turned around, retreating all the way back to the junction I had left forty-five minutes before.

I followed the unmarked trail for about a mile before hitting another trail junction. I looked it up on my map and was utterly disappointed. I had been hiking for over three hours now, and, according to the trail sign, was still eight miles from the top of the rim. My body was weary, being rundown from the long drive and now the burden of the heavily supplied pack on my back.

I was only a mile and a half from Pine, if I took the side trail back. I decided to change my route and avoid the Arizona Trail. I would hike back roads instead, as this would allow me to lighten my pack load and access water at more frequent intervals. I feared finding myself twenty miles out in the wilderness with no water. I ended the day just a few miles north of where I had started.

~

I was sitting in the small town of Strawberry, Arizona, preparing to head for Camp Verde. I was unsure if I could make it in one day, so I again loaded five quarts of water and started out on a Forest Service road.

I had gone about five miles when I reached a warning sign. The road ahead was extremely dangerous according to the sign. A few minutes later, I was standing on the edge of a hairpin turn, and a cliff. The canyon floor was 1,800 feet below; I could see several mangled, burnt piles of metal at the bottom, the remains of several cars that had not made the turn.

The canyon walls are painted deep red and brown with some white occasionally splattered in. I hiked all the way down to the bottom of the canyon, reaching it around noon. I stopped for lunch next to the crystal-clear Fossil Creek. Had I known it was there, I certainly would not have carried so much water.

After lunch, it was time to climb out of the canyon, a 1,100-foot climb up the other side. I spent several hours winding around the cliff walls, looking down into other impressive canyons. The world belonged to me, except for the occasional car that came creeping by. I was impressed by how quickly the landscape changed from pine forest to desert. Cactus were everywhere, as were beautiful purple and yellow flowers.

I reached the end of the forest road around five, emerging at a road sign: "Camp Verde six miles." I had already hiked thirty miles, but felt I could go another six, so on I pushed. I soon could see town down in the valley as I looked out through the clean southwestern air. I hiked down Route 260, which was under construction, a major change from my quiet day in the desert. It was dark by six-thirty, and I hiked the last mile into the edge of town with my headlamp on.

I stopped at the first gas station to get directions to the closest motel. I was tired, and disappointed to learn the only motels were still four miles away, out by the interstate. I had never hiked forty miles in a day before. I wouldn't be able to say that in the morning.

I pressed on in the darkness, grateful to have a wide berm and light traffic. I finally reached the row of motels around nine and checked into the first one. I was thrilled to find it had a Jacuzzi; my worn body could certainly use that.

I woke the next morning to a body in full rebellion. I could barely move! I hobbled to the shower, and slowly my sore muscles began to loosen up. I checked out of the hotel, shouldered my pack, and headed north, but not sure exactly where to.

The Verde River was in my way. There were two bridges, one just north on the interstate and the other three miles south on a road that would not take me where I wanted to go. I chose the interstate. My body was stiff, and walking was a chore. My body was also readjusting to the dry desert air, and I had suffered bloody noses daily since returning west. My feet, shins, calves, shoulders, and knees hurt.

I kept moving and finally reached my exit where I turned away from the interstate, headed for Sedona, some twenty-two miles away. I walked along in the dead, silent air of the desert. Brown mountains ascended majestically from the desert floor all around me. The beauty didn't matter though. I was already feeling lonely. I was a physical and mental wreck.

I stopped about three miles from the interstate to rest my battered body. I was a long way from anywhere, and a long way from nowhere. I didn't feel like walking anymore today. I was not ready to hike several hundred miles alone.

I put my shoes on and walked out to the road. I put my thumb out and the second car stopped. In no time, I was headed back to Camp Verde. The fellow asked where I wanted to go, so I explained everything to him. He then asked if I wanted to go on to Payson. I had not planned to go back that far, but all of a sudden, it seemed like the right thing to do. I could wait for my friend Nomad there. I longed for some company. I took the ride.

Nomad would not be in Payson for a another week, so I decided to tour a little, and to cache a few gallons of water in Southern California, on the longest dry stretches we would be walking. I visited the Grand Canyon, Zion

National Park, Las Vegas, and Joshua Tree National Park, as well as my brother John and a friend in Reno.

They say the third time's a charm, and I was back in Payson for the third time. Nomad arrived, and we celebrated with a good steak dinner, then went back to the hotel to compare notes for which route we would follow. The next morning came way too quickly, as I again did not sleep well. We were off hiking at seven-thirty anyhow.

We headed west out of town, hiking the paved road to the outskirts, where it became a dirt forest service road. As we climbed to the top of the first hill, the Mazatal Wilderness was shown to us. The Tonto National Forest is three million acres and the Mazatal Wilderness is located in the middle of it. I stood in awe as the mountain range appeared to go on forever.

We hiked steadily down from 5,000 feet to the Baby Doll Ranch and the dry East Verde riverbed, which sat in the valley at 3,400 feet. Shortly after passing the ranch, we reach the boundary to the Mazatal Wilderness. There was a turnaround and a gate; no traffic was allowed beyond, except for the owners of the L-F Ranch, the only private landowner within the wilderness boundary. The ranch, like most in these parts, had been in the family for generations and was buried several miles deep into the wilderness.

The day was turning hot, and I felt queasy. Nomad and I trudged along, up the rugged old road. Deep ravines marred the road, and large rocks protruded everywhere. We were sure no one had driven the road in a long time. The surrounding countryside was remarkable, though, filled with cactus-covered mountains and mesas. We were nearly at the L-F Ranch, and our trailhead, when we heard an engine. With unbelieving eyes we watched as an old two-ton, two-wheel-drive box truck crawled across the rugged dirt path towards us. There were two men in the cab, and a cow in the back.

 When they reached us, they stopped. I am sure they weren't used to company. They were both just as happy as could be, seemingly in love with their lot in life. The quiet life on the ranch in this majestic but desolate wilderness was all they needed. There was no electricity and no telephone. A windmill pumped their water.

 "Afternoon, y'all out ta hiking?" the driver inquired.

 "Why, yes we are sir, Quite the place ya got here," Nomad returned. "We are looking for the trailhead. Could ya tell me where it might be?"

 "Well you're almost there, just about another quarter mile up the road. When will ya be back through here?"

 "Aww we ain't coming back, we are going through, all the way to California. We plan to pass through the wilderness; should be at the interstate tomorrow afternoon."

 "Ain't no way you're gonna get through this wilderness in two days. You'll be lucky to do it in four. Going clear to California? Wow! I guess you boys got some time on your hands. Well listen now, the spring ten miles out is running. Ya might have to get a stick and clean the pipe to get water, but she's a good spring, she's a-runnin' alright."

 "Why, thank you very much" we said. "That is good to know. Well, we best get moving, we got mountains to climb."

 As we started to depart the old man offered one more piece of advice, "Now y'all be careful out there. People *die* out there, ya know!"

 As we walked off, we both questioned his ability to judge distance. Four days to get through? Obviously, he had never seen the likes of two hikers like us.

We found the trail and commenced to climb out of the valley, the hot desert sun beating down upon us. I was still not feeling better and after a few miles had to stop to rest. I felt weak and feared I was quickly becoming dehydrated. I thought I might be at an early stage of heat exhaustion. I told Nomad of my concerns, and we both knew the answer was to take our time and go slow. We also knew we had to make it to the first water source, still several miles away.

We finally reached the gap and crossed over to the other side of the mountain we had been climbing all afternoon. We began the descent down the other side, into the valley and to the water source. I was weary and stopped repeatedly for short breaks. I was glad to be going downhill and slowly ambled along, well behind Nomad. My whole focus was on making it to the water source.

I finally heard Nomad give a shout back at me, "Hey I am here, and I found the spring!"

I was soon with him to find a holding tank that was nearly full, and the spring that was not running. We took a stick as instructed and cleaned the pipe, then watched in disappointment as a small trickle of brown sludge dropped out. It was not running.

I normally do not carry a water filter, but had decided to do so on this last leg of the journey. I peered down into the murky water in the holding tank, looking at the algae growing on the sides, and the tadpoles swimming around. I dropped the end of the filter into the water and began to pump, and in no time we had filled our water bottles with pure, clean water. I drank a quart and a half, then refilled my bottles. I set up my tent and crawled in, too tired to eat dinner. Nomad encouraged me to eat something, but I couldn't. I quickly drifted off to sleep, glad to be out of Payson again, and glad to have some company.

I awoke at six-thirty to the sound of rain on my tent roof. I yelled over to Nomad, "Hey what do you want to do?"

"I see no need to hurry. I bet it will pass in a bit. Why don't we sleep another half-hour?" he suggested.

I had no problem with that and quickly drifted back to sleep.

The rain did not last long, and we were packed and hiking by eight. I was feeling much better; a good night's rest and a lot of water was the medicine I needed. We had hiked only a mile when we found Bull Trap Spring Cabin. The spring there was also dry, and the old weathered cabin looked as if it had been around a long time. We stopped inside to eat breakfast and plot our course. We had not gone as far as we had hoped and decided we should ration our food. It looked like it might take three days to get across the wilderness. Perhaps the old man at the L-F Ranch knew more than we thought.

From the cabin, we climbed steadily to the next ridge, discovering several new cacti along the way. We saw our first saguaro, and also became very well acquainted with the jumping cholla.

Each jumping cholla has hundreds of pods on the end of each arm. Each pod is covered with needles, resembling a pincushion. The difference between them and a pincushion is that the pins are barbed on the end, and the sharp end sticks out—not into the cushion. The pods, like leaves, shed in the fall and were laying all over the ground. If you step anywhere near them, they jump and stick into you, with several of the barbs jabbing whatever they touch. The removal process is deliberate, painful, and often bloody.

We each donated plenty of blood as we climbed to the ridge overlooking the Verde River. We stood at our first trail junction. The trail sign, old and weathered, lay broken in pieces at our feet. We picked them up and tried to figure out which way they went on the sign originally, and which way we should go. We knew we had to cross the river and decided to go straight, as opposed to turning left and following the river south.

We followed the trail to the river. I arrived first and immediately stepped into the river and began to drink. As Nomad arrived, he asked, "Hey we gonna treat this stuff? Um, I guess not."

According to the map, a Forest Service road was on the other side of the river, but on the other side of the river was a mountainous cliff. There was no road, but there had to be; the map said so! We searched up and down the river for a safe place to cross, eventually finding our spot and going slowly through the swift thigh-deep current.

Once on the other side, we climbed four hundred feet above the river, dodging the jumping cholla as we went. We stopped. Our only view of the trail ahead was the jagged steep walls of the mountain staring down on us. We looked at each other and Nomad declared, "I don't go backwards."

As the last words from the man back at the L-F Ranch echoed through my head, I replied, "I don't *like* to go backwards. But, I don't think trying to bushwhack through this rugged, unforgiving terrain is our best option. I think today is one of those times we should go back."

Nomad thought a second and consented. We retreated to the river to ford it once again and climb up the 1,000-foot hill we had just come down. We stood once again at the worthless, broken trail sign. The afternoon was slipping away, and we needed to make miles—in the right direction. The problem was, we were no longer sure where we were. We did know that if we continued south, we would hit another service road, at a place called Sheep Bridge.

We had ninety minutes of daylight left as we headed south on the trail. The trail was very well laid out. The scenery around us was breathtaking, with craggy cliffs rising from both sides of the river valley. Saguaro cactus dominated the landscape, along with Manzanita trees.

We made good time and soon crested a hill, from where we could see another old cabin and a landing strip. Neither of the landmarks was on our map.

We were lost.

The sky to our east was black, and it appeared another heavy rainstorm was quickly approaching. We pushed on, reaching the river and finding the cabin—on the other side. Trying to beat the rain, we quickly found a spot and forded the Verde River for the third time that day. We then scrambled up the bank to the safety of the cabin. Inside we found two beds; we were overjoyed by our good fortune.

Later that evening I stood on the porch staring out at the desert. It had been a demanding but rewarding day. I fully realized how easy it would be for people to perish out here. The land is brutally unforgiving, albeit beautiful.

The next morning, we were up and packed at first light. We thought we must be at the second river crossing, with the road back on the other side of the river. We ignored the fact that there was a road on our side of the river leading to the cabin. We ignored the obvious, forded the swift river for the fourth time, and again looked for a forest service road that did not exist. No trail, no road. We knew if we followed the river south, we would find a dam and come out of the wilderness. We set out bushwhacking our way along the riverbank. This worked well until the bending river turned away from us, leaving us no shoreline to walk, only a mountain to climb. I began up with Nomad fifty yards or so behind me. The side of the mountain was made of broken crumbling rock, and footing was slippery. I went slowly, using trees and roots to grab when I could.

I had just reached my hand out to grab the base of a small tree when I saw a bee coming out of a hole, quickly followed by another and then several. I was nearly on top of a ground hive and they were sending the drones out to protect their homestead—and attack me. They targeted my face, I began climbing as fast as I could, swatting at them as I went. I prayed that they were not Africanized bees—or I would surely be dead. As I moved out of the vicinity of the nest, they left me alone and I quickly called out to Nomad to choose another route. I suffered several stings, but otherwise was ok.

We hiked on, summiting peak after peak, each time hoping to get a glimpse of the dam in the distance, but never seeing it. We again suffered numerous bites from the jumping cholla, which stuck into our arms, legs, and clear through our shoes into our feet.

Finally around noon, we got our first break. We stumbled upon a trail. By one-thirty, we had reached the trailhead at Sheep Bridge, where we thought we had camped the night before. Finally, we knew where we were.

We started across the wilderness with only two days of food, and had been in the backcountry for nearly four. We had done well in rationing our supplies, however, and we still had food in our bags.

As we crossed the walking bridge, we met Bob and Dell Wright and their friend Bob Dill. They were excited to see hikers emerging from the wilderness, and we chatted with them for nearly an hour. They fed us lunch and gave us an MRE to enjoy for dinner that night.

Finally on the road we had been looking for all day, we set out for the dam, still thirteen miles away. We reached it at dusk and entered the dam area through the open gate on the eastern side. On the other side, the western gate was locked. We quickly climbed the fence, having no other way across. We pitched our tents on the west side of the riverbank and enjoyed the beans and hotdogs from our MRE. We sat and relaxed for the first time in two days, reflecting back on the intense beauty and remoteness of the Mazatal Wilderness.

The next morning we were up at first light. After a quick jelly sandwich, we began the long, slow, 1,600-foot climb out of the Verde River Valley. We reached the pass around one. From the high plateau, we could see the Superstition Mountains on the southeastern horizon. To our north was the rugged Mazatal Wilderness we had just crossed, and to the southwest lay the desert plains where we were headed.

We hiked to the town of Carefree in hopes of finding a good meal and shower, and perhaps a new tip for my Leki hiking pole. As we reached the first buildings we noticed they appeared to be brand-new and empty. We saw no one outside, other than those driving by in their cars. We hiked on in search of the business district of this modern ghost town, but never found it. There were no power lines, no telephone poles, and no business signs. We finally found a Shell gas station with an old 1950s-model sign hanging in front. We stopped and asked the attendant why the town looked so deserted.

"Local law prohibits signs on the road to advertise business and services. Matter of fact, commercial development is really frowned on here," He informed us.

It was an affluent area, and probably the strangest town I had passed through. There were virtually no services to support the 5,000 residents. We sat in front of the Shell station trying to decide what to do. Nomad had hiked five hundred miles since his last day off, and I was tired, but the only lodging in Carefree was over $150 a night. We decided to call a cab to get a ride into nearby Phoenix, and maybe take a day off there.

The next morning we were sitting at the motel in Phoenix enjoying a wonderful cup of coffee. I wanted to repair my hiking pole, but it was a long way to the closest outdoor sporting-goods store. I decided to call Dodger to have him look in his Appalachian Long Distance Hikers Association directory to see if any members lived in Phoenix. He gave me four names and phone numbers. I read the list of names to Nomad, finally reading the name Second Chance. Nomad smiled and said, "Can't be. I knew a Second Chance, met her in Damascus back in ninety-eight."

"Well, I will just give her a call and see if she knows you," I said while dialing the phone. "Hello, Hello. Umm would this by chance be Second Chance?"

I could hear her voice jump with excitement as she enthusiastically replied, "Why yes, this is her."

I introduced myself and told her Nomad was with me. She had the afternoon free and agreed to come and pick us up.

At three o'clock she arrived and had a joyful reunion with Nomad. We headed off to the local outfitter where I got the parts to repair my hiking pole, and then Nomad asked her, "Where would be a good place for us to take you to dinner?"

She looked at us with a smile, "My house. I am cooking for you guys tonight."

Shari, as she is called outside of the hiking community, served us a feast of fresh salad, homemade garlic bread, sausage, and meatballs with pasta and homemade sauce. Her husband, Mike, was out of town fishing with an old friend, so the three of us sat and talked of life and hiking. Mike made it home later, and we all enjoyed a cup of coffee before Shari took us back to our hotel room. She promised to pick us up in the morning to get us back to Carefree and the trail.

~

After a heartfelt thanks and a hug goodbye, we were headed west. My feet were thankful for the day of rest, and ready to go. We had to make only one turn, onto Route 74, better known as Carefree Highway. After hiking a few miles, I saw a sign for Carefree Highway East, but we wanted to go west. I mentioned this to Nomad and we quickly agreed it must be just ahead. We hiked another mile and a half before realizing we had missed our only turn.

We turned around, knowing we added three miles to our already-long day. Finally, we reached the crossing again and saw the sign to go west. The road remained busy until we reach Interstate 17. After we crossed it, traffic became a rare thing, as did buildings and civilization. We were completely out of the mountains and hiking across the desert floor, having dropped down to 1,800 feet in elevation since leaving Carefree.

It was late in the afternoon when we finally reached our campsite for the night, a narrow patch of land lying next to the fenced-in aquaduct that carried water from the lakes to the desert cities south of us. That aquaduct was our water source, and we needed to get in. I assisted Nomad up and over the fence and he pumped all of our water bottles full. It was dark by the time dinner was finished, and I opted not to set up my tent, but to sleep out in the open, enjoying the desert air.

The next morning, we were hiking by six-thirty, and we'd gone about a mile when I needed to take care of some morning business. I informed Nomad I was going to duck off into the brush for a second. I trotted down into the sandy-brown, brush-covered ravine.

I soon found myself in a most unenviable position. I was in the middle of my task when I heard a rattling sound. I knew exactly what it was; I just didn't know exactly *where* it was. My heart jump-started as I frantically looked around trying to locate the snake. The last thing I wanted to do was move in the wrong direction and further frighten it.

When I finally spotted it, I was barely an arm's length away. I quickly hopped away, then hurriedly finished my duties.

Back out on the road, Nomad yelled to me," Hey, you gotta see this critter."

I arrived to see a tarantula he'd just found. He noticed the shaken expression on my face.

"Sheltowee, you ain't that afraid of a tarantula are ya?"

"No, but I am of the rattlesnake I almost stepped on!" I looked back at the tarantula and added, "I think I will pitch my tent from now on."

"I wondered how long it would take for you to figure that out," he replied, laughing.

The road was quickly wearing my tender feet down, and I stopped after seventeen miles to drain the blisters on each foot. We stopped again five miles later to again relieve the fluid from my swollen feet.

I hobbled into the town of Wickenburg around five-thirty. The fifty-six miles in two days had been brutal on me, and my feet were a disaster area. Just as in Ohio and Oklahoma, my feet rebelled against so much road walking. I needed another day off to let my feet heal.

The next morning, I hobbled uptown to get some compeed bandages to help protect my feet. Nina had advised me to carry some, but I hadn't heeded her advice. Not too proud to be wrong, I was ready to try it.

On my way back, I was drawn into an old tavern named The Bar Seven. Shari had been through and told me not to miss it. The rusted sign out front simply had a seven with a bar over top, an old branding mark I suppose. Inside, I met Wes, a slim, elderly man who was the barkeep. Wes has been tending at The Bar Seven since 1942, the only job he'd ever had. He didn't own the place, he was just a faithful employee. We chatted for a while, and I listened to stories of the other travelers who had passed through, folks on bikes and horses. He had never seen a man walk across the area.

The next morning, I felt good enough to press on and got out of town just ahead of Nomad. A few miles out of town, I reached the site of a famous stagecoach massacre. It was early in the morning in November of 1871, as the stagecoach bounded across the primitive desert road, bound for Ehrenberg. It carried eight passengers, one of them the very well to do Madame Molly Sheppard. It is believed that she was carrying close to $15,000, as well as her large collection of jewelry. She had sold her business back in Prescott, and her reputation was well-renowned throughout Arizona Territory.

Nearby, not far from Wickenburg, a band of raiders came swooping down on the unsuspecting group, killing nearly everyone. Molly and a fellow named William Kruger somehow managed to escape. They fled the scene, and the bandits let them go. Several hours later, when a rescue party went out to reclaim the bodies and what was left of the wagon, they found that Molly's luggage had been the primary target. It had been gone through while nearly everything else was left untouched.

Known as the Wickenburg Massacre, the attack has long been blamed on the Apache, though some still argue that if the attackers had truly been Apaches, there would have been no survivors. To this day, the real attackers remain a mystery.

With my history lesson complete, I was back along the road that followed the old stagecoach route, a much safer road to travel in modern times. I kept a good pace, despite my tender feet. The compeed was helping to prevent further injury, but my feet still hurt deeply. After about nine miles, I stopped to rest. Nomad was well behind me, and after a few minutes I got up and started walking alone again.

While it felt good to stop and take the weight off my feet for a few minutes, standing and walking again was a painful matter. My feet had quickly stiffened, and it was nearly fifteen minutes before I could take a full stride again. Each step, no matter how gentle, felt as if my feet were being beaten again and again. After a while, the pain began to recede, and each step got a little easier until I had finally beat my feet into submission, until the nerves quit sending signals of the pain involved.

I made it another nine miles before I stopping again. Nomad caught up with me, and we walked the rest of the day together. After our break, I had to endure the agony of starting out yet again, and the next half-mile was another brutal torture.

We finished our twenty-seven mile day at the town of Aguilla. The town sits in a valley with mountains to the north and south. We had been in this valley since leaving Wickenburg and would stay in it for several days more. The mountain to the south of town has a large white boulder near the top. We noticed it immediately as we walked towards town. There appears to be a large hole in the top of the mountain. The mountain, like the town, is named Aguilla, Spanish for "eagle eye."

Once in town, we checked into the only establishment there, the Jim Burro Motel, Tavern and Café. There would be no discussion as to where to eat tonight. The agricultural town is an oasis in the desert. The farmers grow melons, cantaloupe, and broccoli, thanks to an intricate watering system.

As we walked into the tavern with our packs on, we were warmly greeted by a host of locals. I felt like a hero as they asked questions about the journey, sitting on the edges of their seats waiting for each answer. We soon were locals too, enjoying dinner with the company of our newfound friends.

The next morning found us sitting back at the little café, where our new friend Nancy from the previous night was our waitress. It was twenty-nine miles to Salome, and I needed to make it that day. I set out ahead of Nomad, wanting to get the painful startup out of the way as quickly as possible.

My feet seemed to get stronger as I covered the first six miles of my day. I saw the military fighter jets that I could only hear the day before. They occupied my mind as I kept looking up whenever I heard the loud rumble of their powerful engines, trying to catch a glimpse before they sped away.

I had completed fourteen miles by noon, without stopping once. Though my feet were healing, I was afraid to stop, knowing the pain involved with starting up again. My water bottle finally ran empty after sixteen miles, and I had to stop to refill it. After taking a short break, I was quickly reminded that my feet, while healing, were not healthy. I hobbled a half-mile, working them loose again, until I could finally walk in full steps once more.

I continued across the high plains that had been home since I left Wickenburg two days before. The area is predominantly agricultural fields, some of them planted in pistachio groves or cotton fields, while others were empty, waiting for the next planting cycle to begin. The open fields provided me with hours of entertainment as I watched the small tornadoes called dirt devils dance across the open fields.

We reached Salome with an hour of daylight to spare—pretty good time for a twenty-nine mile day. It was the last of the high-mileage days we would have to do; after Salome, the towns and water sources would be closer together.

In town, I went through what had become a nightly ritual: shower, and doctor my feet, then hobble to the closest restaurant for dinner. My left foot looked much better, and I hoped I would soon be hiking pain-free.

The next morning, we returned to the same little mom-n-pop restaurant for breakfast. I ordered my standard breakfast, but Nomad was feeling hungry and added a half order of biscuits and gravy to his order. When it arrived, his half order included three full biscuits smothered in gravy.

"Ma'am, this can't be right, I ordered a half order of biscuits."

"Now sir, that is a half order. We figure if we keep you happy, you will return."

Smiling Nomad replied, "Ma'am, if I eat all this, I don't think I'll be able to leave!"

The drizzling rain that had been falling when we walked in had stopped. We bid our host at the motel goodbye and headed out. The mountains to our north were bright and sunny, while the skies to our south were blackened with thunderclouds. We were on the edge of the front. We made it about four miles before the light rain returned.

I was feeling much better but certainly did not want to walk in wet shoes. We made it to a small store set in the small town of Hope. The store had a covered picnic table outside. We stopped there to get a soda and see what the weather would do. The people in the store were very excited to see rain, as it was not a common occurrence there.

The small shower left as quickly as it had appeared. We finished our sodas and resumed hiking. As we reached the edge of town a large sign proclaimed, *You are now beyond Hope.*

I walked almost a mile one morning when I realized I had no hobble; indeed, my feet were on the rebound. I smiled inside, thinking for the first time in several days that I might really get to see the Pacific Ocean.

The afternoon hike was filled with sunshine, quail, and the same constant view of a distant gap between the mountains that would lead us out of this incredible valley. Soon a sign came into view. It got closer and closer with each step until we could finally read it: "Cactus Chicks Mini Mart." Just off the road, sitting alone in the desert was a trailer and a few small outbuildings—the mini mart. We could not pass it up, and walked down to get a Gatorade.

Nomad walked inside to make our purchase while I sat outside inspecting my feet yet again. The proprietors came out to meet me as well. They had quite a setup, selling typical mini mart items as well as arts and crafts. The little roadside oasis seemed out of place, but the two women were happy and content with the freedom that running the desert store provided them.

The next day, it came time to say good-bye to an old friend. After walking over six hundred miles along this highway, I certainly knew the road well. I had set foot foot on the route in west Texas, and now we were nearly in California.

Route 60 ends because the interstate was built, and there was not enough room for both roads to travel through the mountain passes. The next thirty-four miles would be along Interstate 10; the quiet of the desert would soon be replaced with the constant hum of passing cars and trucks.

We had gone no more than a half-mile when we met our first Arizona state patrolman. He was sitting on the berm we were walking down, with a car pulled over. Nomad and I hit our invisible button, hoping to walk by unnoticed.

"Hey guys, don't go too far, I need to talk with you."

Well, I guess that plan didn't work.

"Now guys, you have to know that walking along the interstate is illegal."

"Yes sir, but we could not find any other way through. You see, we have come a long way," Nomad started out, explaining to him about our journeys. "This is *the only* road through here."

The officer looked at us, reading the business cards we provided him. The woman in the car was impatient and got out. He walked away from us and firmly told the woman, "Ma'am just wait in your car, I will be with you shortly. Please get back in your car!"

He walked back to us, smiling. He knew we were not vagrants, and not hitchhiking, but indeed on a great adventure. He questioned, "How long you plan to be walking along here?"

"Sir, we just need to get across the Colorado River. We plan to spend tonight in Quartzite and then should be in California by noon tomorrow."

"Man, I wish you would have invited me. I may very well have come and walked the whole way with you. OK guys, be as quick as you can. I didn't see you."

Three hours later, after waving to seemingly a million cars and choking down gallons of exhaust fumes, we reached the Quartzite exit. We were just off the ramp and on the road into town when a small car came by us. The guy inside looked a lot like Nomad and was waving enthusiastically at us. He passed us and then stopped to turn around.

"I think he believes you're his long lost brother, Nomad," I said with a smile.

He passed us again and pulled over as soon as he found room, quickly getting out of his car and waving yet again.

"Sheltowee, I am not sure who he is, but I do know he is a hiker."

When we reached him he asked, "Nomad, is that you?"

It was Billy Goat, hiker extraordinaire! He recently finished his second hike of the Pacific Crest Trail. He just happened to be passing through the area, and when he saw our hiking poles, he knew we were hikers as well.

Billy Goat drove into town and waited for us at the Silver Spur. We enjoyed lunch and some great repartee of trail days, hiking, and life in general. Between the three of us sitting at the table, we had over 40,000 miles of hiking in. I was the weak link with a mere 7,000 miles.

After another good-bye that came all too quickly, Billy Goat was headed towards Phoenix, and home. Nomad and I wandered into town to find our home for the night. In town, there were only two motels.

"Now remember, Sheltowee, we want a phone that reaches the beds and a bathtub so I can do laundry." We agreed to meet up in five minutes.

"I would just as soon sleep on the ground than pay $51 for a room with no phone," Nomad grumpily exclaimed upon return.

"I take it your little endeavor at the hotel did not go well."

"They want fifty one bucks, and they don't even have a phone, let alone a tub. I ain't gonna pay it! How much was your hotel?"

Grinning, I replied, "You ain't gonna believe this. Fifty-one bucks, no phone no tub. They have one room left."

"Ahhh man, you gotta be kidding. We are on the interstate. I can't believe there is not a motel with a phone here. We had better service in the middle of the desert. Well, I think I may have burned a bridge or two at that motel. Maybe we should go get that last room."

We walked back to the motel I had scouted out, and I again inquired about that last room. It had just been rented.

We ended up saving fifty-one bucks and pitching our tents in a grove of trees behind Burger King. It was our last night in Arizona. I sat in my tent, thinking back on the several hundred miles I had enjoyed in Arizona. From the beautiful pine forests of the White Mountains and the remoteness and intense beauty of the Mazatal Wilderness, to the Saguaro Cactus, roadrunners and tarantulas of the desert, Arizona had far surpassed all of my expectations.

California

We were up at first light and off to McDonald's for a quick breakfast, then back out to the interstate for the last seventeen miles of Arizona. The traffic was already humming by, and I quickly got into a good three-mile-per-hour rhythm. Nomad and I were again celebrities, as nearly every person passing by waved or honked.

I am amused at how many different ways a person can wave. There is the common hand wave, where a person gently waves the hand back and forth. Then there is the excited common hand wave, which is the same motion, but much faster. Some folks bob their head, along with the wave, as if their head and hand cannot operate independently of each other. Some bob a little while others will nearly touch the steering wheel.

Some folks lift one finger—that is the whole wave—just a simple acknowledgement with the index finger. Some lift two fingers to make a peace sign, and still others lift all four fingers, leaving the thumb wrapped around the wheel for control.

Some folks will wave with their non-driving hand out the window. Some will toot their horns, and some will double toot. Then there are those who want to make sure you see them and just lay on the horn until they are past. Most who passed were smiling, cheering us on.

The seventeen miles passed quickly, and we crossed the Colorado River and entered California early in the afternoon. In town, we passed the local American Legion, of which I am a member. We decided to stop and get directions for a place to stay.

Inside the Legion we met Cindy, who lived in Palo Verde, the next day's destination. She knew the owner of the small five-room motel in Palo Verde and called to reserve us a room. We spent an hour talking with the local veterans, and the next thing we knew they'd convinced Nomad that he, too, should be a Legionnaire. He filled out his application and is now a proud member of the Blythe, California, American Legion.

The next day was spent hiking between the roads and dirt banks of the irrigation canals, watching the crop-dusting planes and helicopters fly back and forth. The gravity-fed irrigation canals take water from the Colorado River. The water winds through miles of canals, and what is not used is eventually routed back into the river. The system turns this arid desert land into some of the most fertile farmland in all of America.

We hiked past numerous fields of cotton and alfalfa. The alfalfa is a constantly growing crop, grown to feed livestock. The hay fields back home in Ohio generally get two cuttings each year. If the farmers are lucky, they will get a poor third cutting late in the fall. In the southern California desert, they are able to get seventeen cuttings on the alfalfa fields each year. The first step is to flood the field, then wait three weeks. The sun is ever present here, and after three weeks the field is ready to be cut. After cutting, the field is again flooded and the process repeated, year round.

We stopped in the small town of Ripley to enjoy a hot homemade burrito for lunch. We then continued hiking south through the bountiful Palo Verde Valley, the Palo Verde Mountains looming on the horizon. The landscape had changed drastically from Arizona. We left the Saguaro cactus behind, as they grow only in Arizona. In return, we discovered palm trees. It is remarkable how green everything is in the desert valley.

All things have a price, however, and the price of farming and large cities in the western desert lands is the robbing of waters from the rivers. The Rio Grande has been the lifeblood of much of the west for centuries. Today it is in trouble. The river has always flowed into the Gulf of Mexico; today it usually runs dry before reaching that far. It is often dry before it ever gets to Mexico, and when it is able to sustain itself into its southern ranges, the water that flows there is a toxic mixture of agricultural runoff and sewage.

The Rio Grande ecosystem is dying before our very eyes, and we are allowing it. Eighty percent of fish species unique to the Rio Grande have become extinct in the past century. More than two thirds of the water taken from the Rio Grande is used to grow crops to feed cattle. The antiquated irrigation systems in use are inefficient and continue to overtax the river system.

In New Mexico, Albuquerque's thirst for water is leading it to bring water in from the Colorado River, several hundred miles away. The Colorado River was the last river in America to be completely mapped, long remaining a wild, free-flowing river. Its power is evident through the magnificent Grand Canyon as well as Glen Canyon, though Glen Canyon can longer be enjoyed. Teddy Roosevelt had commented on the Grand Canyon, "...the ages have been at work, and man can only mar it." His fear was realized in the early 1960s when five million yards of concrete were poured to dam the Colorado River, and drown Glen Canyon, one of America's treasures.

The damming of Glen Canyon has been called the most stunning assault on wilderness America has ever seen. Lake Powell can store 27 million acre feet of water, the equivalent of 27 million football fields covered by one foot of water. The hydroelectric power plant provides less than three percent of the Southwest's energy needs; its sole purpose is to fund the development of other smaller dams. Not a single drop of water from Lake Powell is currently used for commercial irrigation, and the restricted flow of water continues to destroy the Colorado River ecosystem. It is believed that modern, more efficient irrigation systems could free up five million acre feet of water every year, more than enough to fuel the projected growth rate for the next 150 years.

Glen Canyon can be saved if we drain Lake Powell. There is a strong movement to do just that, as the struggle for water rights and environmental balance continues to concern our leaders and citizens.

Nomad and I reached the small town of Palo Verde that afternoon. The locals at the Lagoon Lodge were awaiting our arrival. We enjoyed a hearty dinner at the saloon while making several new friends.

The next morning I was out ahead of Nomad, again walking the irrigation ditches and enjoying the late fall desert weather. I finally passed the last of the canals and began to climb towards Palo Verde Peak. The road was busy with trucks hauling hay and alfalfa to the cattle yards. We had seen many of them for the past several days, and they had come to know us, honking their horns each time they passed by.

We hiked an uneventful twenty-four miles to reach an empty border patrol station. It was Nomad's birthday, so I carried a couple of fried cherry and apple pies to celebrate the occasion. After dinner, I pulled them out and we sat laughing and enjoying the freedom of being hobos.

Nomad pitched his tent and was settled in for the night. I decided to sleep in the open air once again, and was off to the side of the building under a small pavilion. I had just crawled into my sleeping bag when a car pulled up.

I watched as three border patrol agents stepped from the car and walked towards the building. As usual, I was not hiding and decided to let my presence be known with a cheery, "How ya doing tonight?" As usual, I startled my unsuspecting company and one of them quickly waked towards me.

"You alone out here?"

"Nah, my hiking partner is camped behind the building."

"What are ya doing here? How did you get here?"

With that, I gave him the short version of the hike. He was satisfied with the answer and walked away to check out Nomad. I watched him disappear into the shadows behind the building and then scream. I sat laughing, knowing darn well that Nomad had also said hello and scared the poor fellow.

The three of them never did go in the building; they just got back in their car and zoomed off. I guess their work could wait for another night.

Our journey the next morning led us past an endangered desert turtle sanctuary. It is a very large facility, covering what must be thousands of acres. The entire facility looks more like a turtle prison than a sanctuary, as an eight-foot high fence topped off with a rolled razor wire fence on top surrounds it. I guess they didn't want them climbing the fence to get out. I saw no turtles, but did see the posted signs every hundred yards warning that it is a felony to touch or harass them.

I finally caught up with Nomad at the Glamis Beach store. An oasis in the middle of nowhere, the store serves the hundreds of thousands who come to play in the Imperial Sand Dunes National Recreation Area, which lay just ahead.

The place was bustling with people on motorbikes, ATVs, and dune buggies. We talked with a group of the riders, discussing our adventure and their hobby.

It is not a cheap hobby: a high-tec buggy costs 40 to 60 thousand dollars, and some go for over 100 grand. They are powerful machines with many of them commanding over 300 horsepower to propel the 650-pound vehicle across the sand. Each of them comes equipped with wheels that have scoops built into the rubber to dig into the sand to glide atop the beach.

With the lunch break over, we bid our new friends goodbye. It was time to see the massive sand dune up close. The area was once the bottom of a large lake, which dried up about five hundred years ago. Today the mound of sand stretches forty miles north and south and is nearly six miles across. The area is divided by Route 78, the south side being open for the buggies, the northern half set aside as a preserve for the natural area to exist undisturbed.

The landscape is ever changing as the winds blow the sand into different mounds, some as high as three hundred feet. A rare sand grass lives here, as well as kangaroo rats. The hydration system of the kangaroo rat is so efficient it never needs to drink water. It receives all of its water needs through the vegetation it eats.

We spent the next few hours watching the hundreds of sand vehicles climb up and down the sand hills, as we made our way across the seemingly infinite sea of sand on foot. We were glad to have the pavement of Route 78 beneath us, making the walk across much easier than it would have been otherwise.

The mountains we had just hiked through surrounded us to the north and east. To the west lay the Imperial Valley, a vast expanse of flat desert farmland. As I continued to walk west, I saw several US Navy F-18s diving towards the desert floor, completing practice bombing runs in the bombing range that also lay ahead. They weren't dropping anything, just practicing the flight pattern, dropping several thousand feet, and then quickly climbing out, the roar of the engines a testimony to their power.

We were nearly across the dunes when a truck pulled over and two guys jumped out. "Hey there guys, you have been walking awhile it seems. I bet you're thirsty. Want a Corona?"

A hand delivered ice-cold Corona in the middle of the desert seemed too good to be true. We quickly accepted the offer and sat to talk with Dick and Kelly, who had driven in all the way from Phoenix to participate in the opening weekend at the dunes.

We eventually reached the western edge of the sand dunes, and the ranger station. It is much to hot to ride in the summer, so winter is the busy season for the dunes. This was indeed the kickoff weekend and more than one hundred thousand people were expected to attend the party.

Not wanting to camp at the overcrowded campsite in the sand, we pushed on, out of the dunes and into the southern edge of the bombing range, where Route 78 passes through. I was amused at the security of the bombing range. Every fifty yards or so was a sign, written in English and Spanish, warning of the existence of the bombing range, warning people not to go into the area.

The turtle sanctuary gets an eight-foot high fence with rolled razor wire on top. The warnings there inform everyone that trespassing, and harassing the turtles from outside the fence is a felony. If convicted of harassing the turtles, you would lose your right to own a gun, to hunt, and possibly to vote. Evidently, it is not a felony to trespass on the Naval bombing range, and the posted notices are all that is needed to keep people out, which is probably true, but the disparity between the two security systems seemed odd to me.

The next day we dropped down from the plateau of the dunes into Brawley, California, which lies below sea level. The irrigation canals reappeared about twelve miles east of town, as did the green fields of the desert farms. Along the way we were passed by thousands of cars, each towing its favorite sand toy, headed for the big weekend kickoff.

In town, we walked to the first hotel we saw and got a room and our first shower in three days. I sat in the room, amused at the fact we would have to hike uphill to reach sea level, when I heard a knock on the door.

It was Dodger grinning ear to ear. He was supposed to meet us in a few more days and provide us a ride back east, but he had grown restless and decided to come early. He knew what town we would be in but had no idea where in town we would be.

After we were settled down a bit I just had to ask him, "Dodger, just how in the world did you find us?"

"It was easy, I just thought like a hiker. I drove into town and looked for the first hotel. The folks at the desk refused to tell me if you were here though, so I just walked by each room, hoping to find you. I am glad you had left your curtain open."

The next morning was cool, but by mid-morning the heat of the sun was pounding down upon Nomad and I as we hiked due south towards the Mexican border. We again watched military jets and helicopters fly above us, completing their daily sorties. As the F-18s and A-6s flew about me, my mind returned to my days in the Navy, some of which was spent at North Island Naval Station across the harbor from where I would finish the hike.

We passed through the small town of Dixieland. It was so small that the only building I saw was that of the Desert Fox Tavern, which, as luck would have it, was open. Nomad and I sat talking with Michael Desota, the elderly Mexican man who owned and operated the small desert oasis.

"When is the last time y'all had a good rain here?" Nomad asked.

"Well, hmm, rain ya say? Let me think. Hmm. Well I guess it was nineteen..."

My mind immediately began to think what he would say. Would it be nineteen weeks, nineteen months, maybe 1999?

Michael continued, "Nineteen and ummm nineteen seventy-six. Yep, it was nineteen seventy-six, we had a hurricane come through."

We sat and laughed in amazement. We finished our drink and bid Michael a prosperous future, then headed out into the hot, dry, desolate road, continuing to drop farther below sea level.

The next few days passed quickly as we plodded through the desert to reach the Cleveland National Forest and the last natural barrier between us and the ocean. Our last stop before the forest was the small town of Ocatillo. Dodger met us there and made arrangements for us to stay at the only available lodging in town. The only restaurant had closed just before we arrived, so we walked into The Lazy Lizard Saloon in hopes of finding dinner. Inside we met Lynn and Doc.

They asked the normal questions, including why we were carrying ski poles across the desert. Nomad and I had each heard this question a hundred times, and Nomad decided this time he would have fun with it.

"You mean ya ain't heard of *sand castle jumping* yet? Why, it is the fastest growing sport in all of the summer Olympics, and this here desert is the hottest place on earth if you want to sand ski. And talk about dangerous, whew! These here packs we carry, you ain't got no idea what's in here. They are full of nitrous oxide, and when we are out on the slopes, we have a hose that runs from the pack to our shoes. We just push a button and vroom we are off, screaming down the sand slope, eighteen times faster than a regular skier! So these poles, we use' em just like snow ski poles."

I had to turn away, unable to keep a straight face as he continued to yarn his tall tale for a full ten minutes. Lynn had bought the joke only for a minute or so before she realized he was a master. Doc was taken in for quite awhile however, not sure what to make of this most sincere gentleman telling him all about sand castle jumping.

In the end, we all got a good laugh and again made new friends. We were treated to chilidogs and some great company before checking in at the local motel.

The next morning we set out for a twenty-four mile hike along Interstate 8, the only path through the rugged barren mountains of southern California. As I hiked up and through the strewn boulders, I imagined how difficult it must have been to get through here in the 1800s, long before we leveled the ground and made a passageway. Several border patrol cars passed us, but none stopped to check us out.

We passed numerous caches of water, sometimes entire cases of water, left out for the illegals crossing the border. There are footpaths that run all through these hills, all heading south to Mexico, which was just a few miles away. The paths were littered with clothing, left behind because it was too much to carry, or when an illegal had been caught. It was left behind perhaps to keep the next group warm as they sat in the cold desert darkness waiting for a chance to hitch a ride along the interstate. We watched as a border patrol helicopter flew over, back and forth along the border. There are plenty of hiding places in the deep ravines and among the boulders.

I decided that my wonder of how they managed to get through a hundred years ago was silly, as it was apparent that getting through today on foot was feasible. The main concern was dehydration, or even worse, getting caught.

The issue of border security is an issue removed from most of America, but is a very real issue here, and is a humble reminder to the promise that America has always held for so many looking for a better life.

We climbed up a little more than 3,000 feet before we began hiking up and down through the interior of the mountain range, like a ship rolling along at sea. The mountains were nearly as barren as the valley had been below, a desolate landscape that reminded me of Mars more than Earth.

Dodger met us at the end of the day, and took us to the Jacumba Resort and Hot Springs. We enjoyed the soothing relief that only a natural hot spring can deliver, all the while realizing the journey was nearing its end.

We had not hiked very long the next day when the transformation in the landscape just overwhelmed me. Trees began to appear, and on occasion, even a running stream. We hiked on through the Campo Indian Reservation as we descended into Campo Valley. The tree-filled mountains support a healthy bird population, and it was a joy to listen to them chirp as I walked along.

We pulled into the small town of Campo, the first town on the Pacific Crest Trail, just a short distance from the trail's southern terminus at the Mexican border.

We made our way down to the border and the true
beginning of the trail. I looked in the logbook and found
Yogi's name. She and I had hiked the first two weeks
together along the Appalachian Trail back in 1999. I looked
a little longer and found Citrus, another friend I had made on
the 1999 hike. They had both come west to hike the 2,600-
mile long gem of the west coast.

I sat at the marker, the steel wall of the border just
feet behind me. I stared north up the skinny worn trail that
runs endlessly onward to Canada. I was proud that I had
returned and made it this far, but I had not expected the
intense emptiness I was experiencing. This was a major
milestone, as I had originally planned to turn north here, to
hike another several months through the summer. I should
have been here in April, but it was now November first and
going north was no longer an option.

I had no regrets for spending my summer with Nina,
but the urge to go north was there, calling me—begging me
to see what lessons it had to teach me. Indeed, the Pacific
Crest Trail was an adventure I desperately wanted—I *needed*
to experience.

Dodger and Nomad were ready to get moving, so I
set my feelings aside and continued on, leaving Campo
behind—for now.

We camped that night at a local park under beautiful
starry skies. This indeed would be the last night of camping
on the journey; the next day we would reach the outskirts of
San Diego. I lay in my tent trying to remember all that I had
seen and discovered. I'd had high expectations of the
America I had come to find, but what exactly had I found? I
had much to ponder over the last few days of hiking.

The morning started out under beautiful blue skies, as
we began the long descent into San Diego. The mountain
road became very narrow as it twisted and maneuvered

through the tight mountain passes, or hugged a berm, just large enough for two lanes of road. The road had virtually no berm and the morning walk was one of extreme caution; listening for cars around each blind turn, and then clutching the side of the hill to give up every inch of space possible when one did come. Fortunately, traffic was light and we were able to pass out of the mountains and to the outskirts of San Diego by the day's end.

The sun was gone and we hiked into a thick, wet wall of grey. After several miles, our cozy two-lane road became a raging four-lane divided highway loaded with intense high-speed morning traffic. Dodger had scouted the route for us and told us to hike the busy road to the Bancroft exit. We had it in sight when a county maintenance vehicle pulled over to inform us we could not walk along the highway. After a quick discussion, he agreed to let us go the quarter mile on to our exit.

From there, we walked the near empty sidewalks, passing restaurants from every cuisine imaginable—Mexican, Cuban, Taiwanese, Ethiopian, Chinese—the list went on. The rain kept many would-be travelers off the streets, so hiking with a pack through the heart of San Diego was easier than expected.

We greeted the people as we walked by, but generally, we did not get a reply—generally, they looked away from us. Finally, two young boys, perhaps thirteen years old, stopped us and asked what our hiking poles were for. Nomad and I explained in great detail about the poles, and the adventure. It was such a joy to meet two fine young men, so full of curiosity and who were not afraid to say hello to a couple of old hikers. They were the bright spot of my morning.

As I walked off, I thought how their eyes shined, and of the radiant joy that emanated from them. Then I thought

of the eyes of many of the other people I had passed today.
Their eyes showed fear, distrust, and unrest. It was if their
childhood dreams—and the twinkle in their eyes—had
somehow vanished.

As the day's rain continued, I got wetter and colder.
My short pants were drenched, as were my shoes and socks.
My fingers were wrinkled and cold, but my torso was dry
and warm, thanks to my raincoat. We eventually met
Dodger at the entrance to the San Diego Zoo, where he
served as a tour guide through the maze of sidewalks in
Balboa Park. It was a smorgasbord of plant life, museums,
and intriguing architecture. It was still raining and we spent
little time sightseeing. We pushed our way through the park
to reach the end of the day's hike and the warmth of a motel.

We had gone a mere mile the next morning when the
rains returned, light but steady. The fog was thick, and
visibility was limited. We crested a hill, then headed down
several steep rolling drop-offs, much like the terrain of San
Francisco. When we reached the bay, we could see nothing.
The city skyline was no more than a half-mile away, but it
was invisible. We headed north along the bay, passing the
docked CVN-74, the USS John C Stennis along the way.

Our spirits soared as we both were about to finish our
own great adventures of walking across America. As we
crossed onto the peninsula of Point Loma, the rain stopped.
We then turned south and headed for the Old Point Loma
Lighthouse. We passed the National Cemetery along the
way and stopped to pay our respects to our veteran
comrades.

When we reached the entrance to the Point Loma
National Park, we were greeted warmly. We explained the
magnitude of the day and were immediately given free
admission into the park. The ranger, Carol Martin,
congratulated us while informing us her daughter had just

completed hiking the Appalachian Trail. Her trail name was Mountain Fairy.

A few of Nomad's friends also were inside waiting for us, Glen Van Peski and Greg Barnes. It was an emotional time for all, and our small group made its way to the historic old lighthouse. The fog had begun to lift, and I could clearly see North Island Naval Station, where I had served eighteen years before.

The group of tourists present gathered around to congratulate us, each with a hundred questions. Nomad and I embraced and walked into the lighthouse, looking out at the Pacific Ocean. We had indeed made it

All that was left to do was touch the water. The ocean lay several hundred feet below us, and we all convened to walk the last quarter-mile together. We had just begun our descent when Doug Daily, a high school friend of mine who lived nearby, joined us. It was great to see him, and I found myself humbled that he had taken time from his busy day to celebrate with me.

We walked down to the rugged coastline. The storm had the surf up, and it appeared to be high tide as well. The moment was filled with pictures and laughter, and a hollow spot. A feeling deep inside that quietly cries, "you're done," a little question of doubt from within that wonders, "what is next?"

Overrun with emotion, Nomad and I walked out as far as we felt safe, far enough to get salt water on our feet and a have a wave crash over us. Indeed, we could not go any farther west.

That night I finally understood what I had discovered. I had found a friendly, compassionate America that loved an adventurer, an America that was not afraid to stop to say hello, or to offer help even when none was requested.